PROUD AMERICANS
GROWING UP AS CHILDREN OF IMMIGRANTS

• • •

STORIES ABOUT LIFE IN THE USA
By Judie Fertig Panneton

ACKNOWLEDGMENTS

The photograph you see on the front cover of this book is of my mother, Esther, my brother, Jim, and me. The year was 1954. The place was Kingston, Pennsylvania, and my father, William, was the photographer.

It has been both an honor and a challenge to grow up in America as a child of immigrants. I have learned from many of the people I have had the privilege to interview that I'm not alone in feeling that way. Thanks to all of them for digging deep to share personal stories about their coming-of-age in this wonderful country.

To my husband, John, and daughters Leah and Haley, thank you for your support and advice along the way to publication. I couldn't have done this important work without you by my side and cheering me on.

Thanks to my friends who have encouraged me, with a special nod to Andrea Hurst and Suzette Riddle who have believed in this project from the start.

Appreciation also goes to Deborah Pacyna, Amberly Finarelli, Al Harrington, the CreateSpace team, and Robin Martin for sharing their talents.

To Dan Poynter, thanks for your invaluable advice and to the late author Frank McCourt, who inspired me during a brief conversation when he asked,"What's wrong with the truth?"

Most importantly, thanks to my parents, who sacrificed so much to come to America.

INTRODUCTION

by Kevin Johnson

Mayor of Sacramento (named America's most diverse city by Time magazine), philanthropist and former player for the Phoenix Suns

Children of immigrants are among the best, brightest, most talented and driven people I have had the privilege to know. I have witnessed their strong work ethic, idealism, family loyalty, appreciation of their heritage and cultures as well as their profound love for the United States.

When you read about the people in *Proud Americans: Growing Up As Children of Immigrants,* you will learn about their personal and families' joys and struggles and how they have been shaped to become the individuals they are today.

Thanks to author and child of immigrants, Judie Fertig Panneton, we get a glimpse into the lives of those who are part of America's Melting Pot; its ever-growing modern mosaic.

You'll "meet" people like Tony Xiong, whose dream is to become a police officer in spite of violent family members. Who would have predicted that he would have had such a dream after growing up in a home where two gang-member brothers were often in trouble with the law?

Then, there's Natalia Estrada, a hair stylist who came to the U.S. Illegally as the daughter of Mexican immigrants who were farm workers. She shares how she didn't want to be the child of immigrants and fantasized about having American-born parents who were white. Estrada's coming-of-age wisdom shows how she grew to become a proud Mexican American.

Dorothy Mitsu Takeuchi remembers growing up as the child of Japanese immigrants and when her family was forced to live in internment camps in the United States. In spite of the hatred and discrimination she witnessed, Takeuchi harbors no resentment and shares some good memories as well as the bad.

Brothers Hani and Maher Ahmad know what it's like to have people call you names because of the color of your skin or the sound of your last name. Both work against discrimination and are proud Americans.

There are also some "high profile" people featured in the book, too, like surgeon and TV host, Dr. Mehemet Oz, whose parents are from Lebanon; Leon Panetta, the former Director of America's Department of Defense and a son of Italian immigrants; Chicago Mayor Rahm Emanuel, the son of an Israeli father; actor Jennifer Anniston, whose parents are Greek; singer Christina Aguilera, whose father is from

Ecuador and whose mother is Canadian; and Steelers player Hines Ward, the son of a Korean-born mother and an American-born father.

As you can see, children of immigrants come from all walks of life and their families' roots stretch into many different directions.

I'm proud to say they are an important part of America and Sacramento's diversity and my life, as well. They have made our communities and our country better places to live and work.

I know I have gained a greater appreciation for this special group of people from reading *Proud Americans: Growing Up As Children of Immigrants* and I know you will, too.

TABLE OF CONTENTS

MAKING
A DIFFERENCE

LEON PANETTA

"Local Boy Does Good," read the April 28, 2011 *Monterey Herald* headline when Leon Panetta was nominated by President Barack Obama to lead the U.S. Department of Defense after serving as director of the Central Intelligence Agency.

Panetta is the son of Italian immigrants, and he mentions it in the many speeches and interviews he gives.

Ever-proud of his heritage, Panetta grew up in Monterey, California in a neighborhood he says was known as Spaghetti Hill because of the many Italians who lived there.

Monterey had been the sardine capital of the world, and the fishing industry and factory work attracted Italian immigrants to the area. "The neigh-borhood was mostly Italian, so I had a strong sense of belonging," Panetta tells me. "I always had a lot of Italian friends to play with and to walk with to the Catholic grammar school we attended."

Panetta's parents owned seven restaurants on the Monterey Peninsula, including one in downtown Monterey, which was named Carmello's Café after his father. He says his mother worked the café's cash register and his father was the chef. Panetta helped out, too. "My earliest recollection of the restaurant was when I was 5 years old," he says. "My job was to wash and rinse the dirty glasses and dishes. I felt proud to be helping my parents work hard."

Panetta says being a hard worker was an important value in his home while he was growing up.

After his parents sold the café, he says they bought 12 acres of land in the Carmel Valley, and Panetta helped his father and his grandfather plant walnut trees. He says his father taught him how to use a hammer and nails, and they worked together with carpenters to build a house on the walnut orchard land. It's a house that he and his wife, Sylvia, call "home" today. "When I look at the driveway and decorative rock, I remember seeing my father and grandfather doing all of the work so many years ago, painstakingly stacking the bricks and rocks, one by one," he tells me. "They would talk Italian and laugh and would never complain about the hard work that was involved."

In addition to working hard, Panetta says he and his brother were expected to succeed in school. "My parents always encouraged us to speak English at home, even though we knew Italian, and they wanted us to get a good education so that we would be successful in this country," he says. "'Make us proud,'" my father would tell us. "'That's why we left loved ones in Italy and came to America: to give you and your brother a better life in a land of opportunity.'"

Panetta says his father wanted him to become a dentist while his mother had hoped he'd be employed as a concert pianist. "'A profession will give you security,'" he remembers his father instructing, as well saying, "'You will need money. Be secure; be your own boss; and be independent.'"

Panetta says after he got involved in student government in high school, he decided to become a lawyer.

A strong, motivating factor throughout Panetta's life has been his parents' desire to make a better life for their family. "That's the main reason why I went into public service," he says. "I remember thinking, 'If a son of Italian immigrants has been able to have opportunities to improve his life, why can't I help give others that opportunity?'"

When Panetta was elected to Congress in 1976, his father was there to see him take the oath of office. Unfortunately, by that time his mother had passed away. He served eight terms in Congress and has held a variety of high-ranking public service jobs, including being director of the U.S. Office of Civil Rights, as well as serving in the U.S. Army from 1964 to 1966.

When he worked as President Clinton's Chief of Staff in the mid 1990s, Panetta says his ability to speak Italian came in handy. He translated President

Clinton's English words into Italian for a large audience in Vatican Square during a visit to meet with the pope.

The father of three sons, Panetta says his children, one of whom is a doctor and two of whom are lawyers, have learned the important lessons his family lived — having self-discipline, working hard, being honest, and remembering that life isn't a bowl of cherries.

Panetta and his wife Sylvia founded the Panetta Institute for Public Policy at California State University, Monterey, and they have been married for more than 50 years. "Each and every day, I am thankful for the life we have built and for being the son of Italian immigrants," he says.

᯼

DR. ERNIE (BALAZS) BODAI

Dr. Ernie Bodai is an inspiration to many – a highly respected surgeon, the brains behind the breast cancer fundraising postage stamp, a nominee for the Congressional Gold Medal of Honor, a cancer survivor, and the author of several books. Yet, Dr. Bodai remembers feeling like an underdog when he grew up in this country as a son of Hungarian immigrants.

It's a theme the 58-year-old Sacramento resident often touches upon in the many speeches he gives throughout the world. He hopes that by sharing his story, others will be inspired and catapulted toward their dreams, no matter where they live and no matter who says they can't.

Dr. Bodai was 8 years old when his family came to the United States. What happened before their arrival has played a major role in the American life he has created.

Dr. Bodai was born in Budapest in 1951 and at the age of 6, his family went into hiding during a Russian invasion. He remembers racing to a cramped bomb shelter with his 8-year-old brother Conrad, his parents, and about 12 strangers. "It was freezing, damp, and miserable, about 20 cubic meters in size," he recalls like it was yesterday. "My mother would rub my hands and blow her warm breath on them to keep them from turning blue and freezing. To this day, I believe she must have had a sixth sense that mothers have, knowing how important my hands would be when I grew up."

Dr. Bodai tells me he'll forever be grateful for his parents, Conrad and Cornelia. They provided protection and showed bravery during those difficult times. He remembers an instance when his father put his life in danger by sneaking a chicken past the authorities to supplement the lard sandwiches and water they ate for six months. "Each day provided its own gifts," he recalls, "especially the gift of escaping from the Communists and moving to the United States."

Dr. Bodai speaks of great admiration for his father, a nuclear physicist, who could have helped the Communists with his PhDs in nuclear physics and mathematics but chose to escape. "He wanted to raise his children in a land of opportunity, where we would have personal and religious freedom and not be forced to join the Communist Party," Dr. Bodai adds.

To a graduating class of medical students at the University of California, Davis, Dr. Bodai once challenged, "Imagine, if you can, the courage it took to leave his native country, his relatives, his education, a potentially lucrative career, and travel to a land where he did not speak the language, his professional degrees would not be recognized, and discrimination in all of its ugliest forms would weigh against him. A hero is a man who does what he can. My father was a hero."

Dr. Bodai remembers the family's arrival in the United States and the sacrifices his parents made to feed and house him and his brother.

"When I was 8, we arrived in Ithaca, New York without a penny in our pockets, only the clothes on our backs, and no comprehension of the English language or cultural complexities of this new world," he says. "We felt alone, desperate, scared, and hopeful, all at the same time."

Without money for day care, Bodai's parents took their two boys to job sites with them to watch them clean houses, lay bricks, and do other menial and physical jobs. "You can't imagine how much it hurt me to watch them work so hard for so little!" Dr. Bodai says. "It also motivated me to become successful because I vowed as I watched them that I was never going to have to work like that, and I was going to be in a position to take care of them, if they needed my help."

About three years after arriving in the United States, Dr. Bodai's parents welcomed his little brother Joey into the family, and it became a life-altering moment. "As I saw my recovering mother and my newborn brother being wheeled by us, I was struck by an epiphany," he remembers. "I wanted to be a doctor!"

And that's where the underdog part comes in. Dr. Bodai had been teased about his second-hand clothes, his "broken" English, and his Hungarian name, Balazs, when he attended grammar school in Southern California, where the family moved for job opportunities. Dr. Bodai was able to change his name from Balazs to Ernie. "It made life a little easier," he remembers, even though it didn't even the playing field.

He also recalls seeing his classmates eating warm cinnamon toast when they were dropped off at school, while he had nothing to eat for breakfast. And forget about inviting friends over to hang out after school because the Bodai tenement apartment was run-down compared to his friends' houses in Arcadia, an affluent suburb.

When Dr. Bodai dreamed of attending a premier high school, like his classmates would, teachers predicted he wouldn't get in and insinuated it was because he was "lesser than" — an immigrant and a child of immigrants. The same thing happened to him when he aspired to attend the University of California, Los Angeles and the University of California, Davis School of Medicine. Not to be dissuaded, Dr. Bodai applied, was accepted by all, and earned degrees. It wouldn't be the last time he was told he couldn't achieve a dream or the last time he proved the naysayers wrong.

While in medical school, Dr. Bodai's parents divorced and he tried to pick up the pieces. Every Friday afternoon, he drove 450 miles to Los Angeles to protect his 11-year-old brother Joey from their father, who had become an alcoholic and had suffered from depression, hallucinations, and nightly blackouts.

The long absences adversely affected his grades and class attendance. During a meeting with the dean of the medical school, Dr. Bodai explained his situation, and the reaction was more than he expected. "If I give your dad a job here at the medical school, would he take it?" Dr. C.J. Tupper asked.

"Are you kidding?" was Dr. Bodai's first response.

Not only did Dr. Bodai's father move to Davis to repair instruments at the medical school, he stopped drinking, reclaimed his life, and joined his son on stage when Ernie Balazs Bodai received his diploma and became Dr. Ernie Balazs Bodai. "Somehow, I feel he got back that little piece of paper — that is, the diploma — that he had left behind in Hungary some 40 years before," Dr. Bodai says. "He left his behind for me and so I gave my diploma back to him."

Dr. Bodai also gave back to the United States and to 12 other countries, including Hungary, by pushing for the sale of a postage stamp to benefit breast cancer research. The idea came to him because of the 500 breast-cancer-related operations he performed each year. Dr. Bodai knew research was key for this non-discriminating disease that strikes about one in seven women. Even though he had been continuously turned down by the federal government for the stamp's approval, Dr. Bodai refused to take "No" for an answer and his persistence paid off. Now, the stamp has raised about $50 million in research funding in the United States alone. "My hope is that one day, research will determine a way to prevent and cure breast cancer," he says.

In addition to his work on behalf of breast cancer patients, Dr. Bodai is an inventor of medical devices, which have saved lives. One example is a device to help premature infants breathe. Much to his delight and surprise, Dr. Bodai saw it in use in a Hungarian neonatal unit while taking a tour of the facility. "It was so cool to see something I did reach back to my native land!" he recalls. "When I saw it, my spine was tingling."

It wasn't the only time that Dr. Bodai had returned to Hungary. He had gone there after his father passed away to carry out one of his dad's last wishes: taking some of his ashes to Hungary to be buried with the grandparents that were left behind. "It was illegal to scatter ashes in the public cemetery where they were buried, but you know what I did?" Dr. Bodai asks. "I hid them under my jacket to sneak them by the authorities, much the same way as my father hid the chicken under his jacket to feed us."

Dr. Bodai keeps his family's sacrifices alive by sharing their stories with others and by never forgetting how America did become the land of opportunity his parents had hoped it would be. His brothers are professionals, too. Conrad is a dentist and Joey works as a respiratory therapist.

Maybe being an underdog isn't such a bad thing. In Dr Bodai's case, it strengthened his resolve to become the doctor, son, and humanitarian he has been determined and destined to be.

❧

PETE CARRIL

Mention the name Pete Carril to basketball fans and you're likely to see a smile of recognition on their faces, and why not? Carril was inducted into the Basketball Hall of Fame for his coaching skills, including his work at Princeton University, where its basketball team had 13 Ivy League championship wins and school earned 21 postseason tournament bids.

As the son of Spanish immigrants, Carril is a no-nonsense coach who believes that having a top-notch character is as important as, if not more important than, getting the ball into the hoop. A former high school teacher, Carril often asks the basketball players he coaches a question his father had asked and that has stuck with him: "What do you stand for?"

Soft-spoken with a hard line on good behavior, Carril used to tell his Princeton basketball players that their parents shouldn't go to sleep having to worry that their children were doing some things they couldn't be proud of.

For about 13 seasons, Carril worked as a "basketball development coach" for the Sacramento Kings.

I met Carril in Sacramento at a fundraising event for finding a cure for juvenile diabetes. He was sitting on a hotel couch, dressed in a black tuxedo, chatting with my husband John, who had been awaiting my arrival. "Judie, I'd like you to meet Pete Carril, one of the greatest basketball coaches that has ever lived," my sports-nut husband said with pride in his voice.

While my eyes did not light up with recognition of the name, they did when Carril told me he was the child of immigrants, and like me, grew up in eastern Pennsylvania.

Born and raised in Bethlehem, Pennsylvania, Carril remembers living in a third-floor apartment building that was owned by the Bethlehem Steel Company where his father worked. "There were about 200 families in that apartment building and just about everyone spoke Spanish," Carril recalls. "There were Spanish, Portuguese, and Mexican families that lived there because of the work at the steel mills."

Carril's father worked at a hot, open hearth, and memories of his return home are described in Carril's book, *The Smart Take From the Strong* (a title based on one of his father's quotes). "He was always coming home with burns on him and me and my sister would rub butter or lard on his skin," Carril wrote. "He drank hard whiskey, a lot of it, but he never missed a day of work for sickness....He deserves a lot of credit for insisting that his children did not wind up the way he did."

"'Use your head,'" Carril remembers his father saying in Spanish to him and his sister while racing out the front door for a day of work at the steel plant.

Carril says his father's English was rudimentary, while his mother had more of a command of the language. "My dad used to make fun of his own English," he tells me. "I saw the furnace where my dad worked and I was told that he was good at what he did."

Carril adds that a big influence in his life growing up was the Boys Club of Bethlehem. He also credits his basketball coaches from junior high, high school, and college for pushing him, inspiring him, and helping him succeed in life. "Athletics have been a help to the lower classes throughout the history of this country," Carril says.

"Families today are not as close as they used to be," Carril laments. "That's why young people get into more trouble today."

He also shares that people have easily forgotten the sacrifices others have made for Americans' freedoms. Carril says he appreciates his parents' sacrifices and identifies himself as an American of Spanish descent.

When he's not coaching in Sacramento, Carril lives in Princeton where his daughter, son, and grandchildren reside.

∾

DR. LOUIS VISMARA

Dr. Louis Vismara, a Sacramento cardiologist, may not be a household name, but the work he has done on behalf of autism is internationally renowned. He is the father of four children, including Mark, who has autism. Dr. Vismara has been propelled to become an advocate on behalf of those with autism, including being the co-founder of the MIND Institute at the University of California, Davis – a collaborative international research center and informational resource for autism and other neurodevelopment and learning disorders. He is also a health-related policy consultant for the California State Senate.

Dr. Vismara was not born in the United States, but he did come here at a young age. He lived in Italy for the first five years of his life, and then moved with his grandmother to the United States to join his mother and father. "My parents came to the United States right after World War II, in large measure because my father was disturbed by what was happening," Dr. Vismara explains. "He was very against the fascist government there and the resulting financial and political turmoil and chaos....They faced danger and adversity and feared for their lives on a daily basis."

When Dr. Vismara's parents came to the United States, they settled in Logan Heights, a diverse neighborhood in the San Diego area, where his engineer father ended up working first as a janitor, then a chemist, and years later, started his own plating company. His mother started earning money in America as a seamstress, and attended the University of California, San Diego, where she earned a degree that enabled her to become a teacher.

"We never felt poor in the United States," he adds. "My parents taught me that this was the land of opportunity and with time, dedication, and hard work, we could achieve our goals and dreams."

Dr. Vismara says that when he started kindergarten at a local public school, he immediately was at a disadvantage because he spoke only Italian, while most of his classmates spoke English. He says he wore short pants and they wore long ones. "I hated the first day of school because you had to stand up, give your name, say what you did for the summer, and where you were born," he relates. "I don't remember the exact words, but I was called 'dego' and 'wop' and whatever."

He adds that it would have been easier to be more Americanized without parents who spoke with heavy accents. "Most kids do not want to be different," he explains.

Named Luigi at birth, Dr. Vismara says he changed his name to Louis when he turned 16, which made his life a bit easier.

Even though there was much Italian culture available in San Diego when he was growing up, Dr. Vismara says his family shunned it. "My parents did not have Italian friends," he tells me. "When I look back in retrospect at it, I think that was pretty sad because that was part of our identity."

When I ask Dr. Vismara if he regrets that lack of connection, he responds, "I don't feel cheated by it. The gift of it was that I could establish my own identity."

One way Dr. Vismara says he accomplished that was through his intellect and musical ability. "My parents made me start taking violin lessons when I was 5, and when I was about 15 years old, my teacher had me try out for the San Diego Symphony and I made it."

Education and achievement were themes Dr. Vismara's parents reinforced for their only son. Dr. Vismara remembers his father presented him with a list of colleges that he considered for his son's attendance for medical school. They included Stanford, Harvard, Johns Hopkins, and Yale.

"How did you feel about that?" I inquire.

"It wasn't up for discussion," he answers.

Dr. Vismara earned an undergraduate degree from Stanford and received his medical degree from Baylor College of Medicine.

In addition to remembering parents who guided him toward achievement, Dr. Vismara describes his mother and father as being patriotic, making sure they exercised their right to vote, and having a keen interest in politics and who was running for office. "They really related to American culture and life," he says.

That's something Dr. Vismara can say about himself, as we finish our interview in his office in the state's Capitol building in Sacramento. "I think America is by far an incredible country, considering the aggregate people we have and the aspirations and accomplishments that have been achieved," he concludes.

∾

JIMMIE YEE

As I'm escorted into Sacramento County Supervisor Jimmie Yee's office, I see him seated behind his tidy, cherry-stained wooden desk, making what appears to be some notations on the documents he is reading. "You're just pretending to be busy," I tease as I enter. Yee looks up, surprised, his concentration broken, and upon seeing me he laughs, knowing that my words are friendly. We have known each other for more than 20 years because of my reporting for local newspapers and magazines in which Yee was often featured for his work, mostly as a Sacramento City Council member and Sacramento's acting mayor.

Yee, a civil and structural engineer who helped design some of Sacramento's landmark buildings, is 76 years old, but he looks more like he's in his mid-60s. Yee's mind is sharp and his memories are clear as he remembers what it was like growing up in what he calls the "Skid Row" section of downtown Sacramento. "That's where all the minorities lived," he explains. "Mexicans, Japanese, Chinese, African Americans. We were a good mixture there. We all lived in the same neighborhood. No one said, 'You don't belong here.'"

The youngest of six children, Yee remembers be-ing happy as a child, even though money was tight and his parents worked hard and for many long hours. His father, Yee Chee Shim, came to the United States from China in the late 1920s and once enough money had been saved, Chee Shim could afford to bring his Chinese-born wife, Yee Bau Jung, to America.

Yee says his father worked as a grocer and his mother helped him, in addition to her cannery and laundry employment. Even though they logged 12 hours a day, six and a half days a week at their jobs, they found time for family dinners and holiday celebra-tions. "My parents took good care of us," Yee explains. "I can recall meals together and once in a while, we had a steak. No one could have it for himself. I had a few slices and everyone else had a few slices, too."

The interview reveals that Yee always seemed focused on the positive when he was growing up in Sacramento. "We accepted life as it was," he tells me. "We didn't know any better." Yee brushes aside the memory of needing to use cardboard inside his shoe to cover up a hole that poked through the sole. So what if his mother never learned to speak English? And what about the jobs he worked as a young man shining shoes, and picking vegetables, including onions and strawberries, in California farm fields?

"Was it demeaning work for someone who is so accomplished?" I inquired.

"No way!" he responds, taking umbrage at the question. "When you were trying to earn a few pennies, whatever work you could get, you did it. You didn't think about it being demeaning. I don't think we knew the word. It was a source of income."

Every day during his junior and senior years of high school, Yee drove a delivery truck for a Chinese take-out restaurant. His sense of being lucky to have the job is apparent. "I made 50 cents an hour, and it included a Chinese chow mein dinner and I had lots of tips," he recalls. "Every night at home, I threw my coins into a jug and it added up to quite a pile for my spending money."

Yee grew up at a time when discrimination against minorities was rampant and legal, including a prohibition against owning property. He remembers living on one side of a rented home with his immediate family, and his aunt and uncle lived on the other side. "In our apartment, my parents slept in the living room and the four youngest kids slept in one bedroom and the two oldest slept in the other," he explains. "The toilet was outside on the back porch. I remember the pull chain to flush the toilet. We also had an ice box that we used to store the ice delivered by a man on a horse-drawn carriage."

He learned some of his family's history from siblings. "My older brother was aware of these things and he told me that when my dad bought property, he had to have someone else buy it for him," Yee explains. "My parents did not sit down and tell me these things."

When I ask him about experiencing discrimination, himself, like in school, Yee tells me it wasn't a problem until he went to high school, and even then, he says there was some name-calling, but it wasn't anything he couldn't handle.

He also recalls being discriminated against as a child in connection with a swimming pool across the street from a public park. The privately owned pool was advertised as being opened to the public, but he was warned that the public didn't include minorities. "My friends said not to bother going because we weren't welcome there," he says. "I didn't try. Why go there and get embarrassed?"

Yee remembers that his parents raised their sons with higher expectations than their daughters regarding education and careers, because they valued the work as mothers and wives that they expected their daughters to become when they got married. "That's the feeling I got that was happening," Yee adds. "It was Chinese tradition and culture. I didn't question those things."

He also didn't question the tradition of being expected to attend Chinese language school in grades K-7 after attending public school every day and on Saturdays, as well. Yee admits it wasn't his favorite place to go. "Every day after American school, we went home for a little snack and then it was off to Chinese school from 5:00-7:00 p.m.," he says. "I didn't do too well because I was more interested in playing basketball and played hooky sometimes. I didn't resent going. It was just part of growing up."

While some things were expected of the children in the Yee family, there was little talk from the parents about their lives in China and their decisions about coming to the United States. He says he knows that his mother and father came to the United States for better economic opportunities and a better life overall. "What I do not know is how my parents met or why my grandfather, who came here to visit in the 1890s, decided to send his sons to the United States in the 1920s," Yee says. "Since they didn't talk about it, I didn't ask about it."

That doesn't mean that Yee wasn't curious. When he was 55, he decided to visit the small Chinese farming village, Loo Chōng, where his father and grandparents lived. "Some of my kids went with me. It kind of tells you about your forefathers. It made me appreciate what we have today versus what it was like in the village where they lived without electricity and gas, used a wooden stove, and had an outhouse about 200 yards away from the living quarters."

Like his parents, Yee has six children; four daughters and two sons. When I ask if he has raised the boys differently than the girls, Yee responds, "I am Westernized.

I believe girls are just as important as boys to have an education." Then, he laughs with pleasure when he tells me, "All of my kids have college degrees, and two have two degrees and one has three."

Yee is also proud that his family keeps Chinese traditions alive, like celebrating the Chinese New Year with gatherings and money-filled red envelopes for the children as they wish them good luck in the new year. Yee adds that when his children were married, he and his wife, Mary, hosted traditional pre-wedding receptions where relatives stop by and the bride and groom offer them tea, and in exchange, the relatives give them something of value like money, jewelry, or jade.

As a politician with experience on the federal, state, and local levels, Yee tells me has most enjoyed his work on local issues. He has paid a price for serving in public office, however. He and his wife will always live with the memory of a white supremacist trying to set their home on fire in 1993, shortly after Yee's election to the Sacramento City Council. A Molotov cocktail was thrown through a vacant bedroom window. The home was not seriously damaged, Yee says, but his and his wife's nerves were frayed and their lives were inconvenienced. "The police said they were concerned about my safety and for two weeks after that, my wife and I had to wear bullet-proof vests," he remembers. "After a suspect was arrested,

I asked that the vests come off and the city no longer provide guards at my house because it cost too much. The incident did make me think more about my family's safety, though."

Being a Chinese American is something Yee is proud of, and he has spoken to students and others about how he went from a Sacramento "Skid Row" resident to one of the most powerful people in Sacramento County. "You feel good about being a role model for the younger generation, which can pursue some of the things that were not so easy for us to get into," Yee explains. "I encourage them to do some of the things that I have done and tell them that nothing comes automatically and that you have to work hard and build and support relationships."

Yee added that he's glad his family settled in the United States. "I feel like one of the luckiest people in the world that they came to America!" Yee exclaims.

❧

FAMILY MATTERS

PARYSA GHAZIZADEH

I meet with 23-year-old Parysa Ghazizadeh over a cup of tea at a downtown Sacramento café, in a building where she works as a student legal office assistant for the state of California. Ghazizadeh, who has long black hair, dark brown eyes, and a big smile, is an energetic young woman with a kindness and inner strength that oozes from her as she talks. A recent college graduate, Ghazizadeh dreams about enrolling in law school to possibly pursue a career in criminal law. She tells me that the ability to help people is an important part of sher career choice.

Born in Santa Clara, California, to parents Pary and Farshad from Iran, Ghazizadeh tells me she has an older brother, who is 29, and a younger brother, who is 17, and a 5-year-old half sister from her father's second marriage. (Her parents divorced when she was 10.)

It was her father's pursuit of an electrical engineering degree in Arkansas that brought Ghazizadeh's parents to the United States. "My father came in 1976 when he was 19 and then he brought my mom, who was 22, in 1978," she explains. "People were very unhappy with the government under the Shah of Iran, and a revolution took place shortly after my parents left Iran."

When I ask her about the stories her parents told her about Iran, Ghazizadeh tells me they had very happy memories growing up as children and as teenagers. "They made it sound like it was a friendly, hospitable, happy place when they were young," she says. "I remember hearing a lot about culture and traditions that take place in Iran, like lavish dinners people held during Ramadan. We fast from sunrise to sunset, so dinner time is spent together to enjoy food and company. It's like Thanksgiving every night for 30 days!"

"What about the United States?" I ask her. "What did they tell you when you were growing up?"

"They always told us about how good we have it here, like freedom, laws, and a society that actually gives us a chance to be whatever it is we want to be," she remembers. "They always reminded us that we are really blessed because not everyone is given the opportunities we are given."

Ghazizadeh, who speaks Farsi and English, attended public schools in Santa Clara and Sacramento. She says her public school attendance was a big adjustment for her parents because boys and girls were seated in classes together, which doesn't happen in Iran. "I would have to tell them that it's okay and normal for boys and girls to go to dances," she explains. "It was kind of scary for them but they didn't bar me from going, and they warned me to be careful about who I hung around with," she recalls.

Throughout her schooling, Ghazizadeh tells me she has had friends from many different cultural backgrounds. "I knew I was different than most kids, particularly in regards to my culture, but I never saw that as a bad thing for the most part," she says. "I remember kids always coming to school with 'normal' peanut butter and jelly sandwiches and I would go to school with Persian kabob. They would ask what it was and after they tasted it, they wanted it."

She remembers a time in about fourth or fifth grade when a friend came to visit her home for the first time. Her mother was cooking and took a moment to greet her friend, and Ghazizadeh thought the visit went well. "The next day at school a kid came to me and said my friend told her our house smelled funny," she says. "It was rude, and it really hurt my feelings and confused me because she came from an immigrant family, a Polish one." She also remembers another elementary school experience — an unexpected encounter with twin girls, who were Jewish, in third grade. "I remember it perfectly. I admired these girls. They were really smart," she recalls, and adds that the girls approached her in the school library. "They asked me if I was Muslim and I enthusiastically said that I was. They said they were Jewish and I said that that was cool. Then they said, 'You don't like us and we don't like you,' and then I asked, 'Why don't you like me?'" She says the response was, "That's how it is — you don't like us and we don't like you."

Ghazizadeh tells me she went home in tears and told her mother the story about what had happened. She remembers her mother's strong response: "You like everybody. You can choose to still like them."

The next day, Ghazizadeh recounts that she went to school still admiring the twins, even though they didn't talk to her. "I learned that others can have a problem with you but it's important not to have a problem with them," she says. "It gives you peace of mind and it lets you know where you stand."

That lesson and inner strength have played important roles in her life, especially since Islamic terrorists attacked the United States on September 11, 2001.

"I was a junior in high school when it happened, and almost instantly people would say that it was my people who caused it," she relates. "It was a hard adjustment for me. It would test my patience when people would ask me questions like, 'Do you hate Jews?' or 'Why do you think oil prices are so high?'"

It was especially difficult for Ghazizadeh because she says her parents raised her to be accepting of others, no matter what country their families were from or what religion they practiced.

"When 9/11 happened, I was pumping gas and was wearing a necklace that said 'Allah' [God] in Arabic. I could hear people say, 'There's one of them.' I saw one person who had an American flag on a mini flagpole in the bed of his truck and he said, 'Why don't you go back to where you came from?'"

She says that without hesitating she immediately responded, "I'll pack up my stuff and go back to Santa Clara because that's where I was born! Does that make you feel better? Have a nice day!"

Ghazizadeh tells me the man said nothing, turned around, got into his truck, and drove away. It is an incident that still angers her today, but she is philosophical when it comes to the bigger picture. "I have learned that you can free people from their ignorance by sharing and explaining parts of my culture and religion with them so they understand that we actually aren't that different at all; it's just that we have different traditions."

When it comes to her family's culture and religion, Ghazizadeh says she loves them as well as America's culture. She believes she's in touch with the best of both of these worlds and explains, "As an American, I am driven and successful because I have been taught it's important to go to school and to get a job. My Iranian culture has taught me a level of kindness that I have not seen in other cultures. When we have guests over, we treat them better than our own family because hospitality is so important. The Iranian culture also teaches us to enjoy being around family and friends and I find that refreshing."

She remembers being raised to respect her elders, including being expected to get up and greet her father when he came home from work. It brings up a memory from her childhood, when she was visiting a friend's home. "I went to her house when I was in elementary school and she yelled at her mom and told her to shut up," she says. "I was sitting in her room and I thought it was just horrible!"

As Ghazizadeh dreams of her future career plans, there is at least one thing about which she is certain. If her parents ever become incapable of caring for themselves, she wants to be able to take care of them. "I was talking to my 17-year-old brother the other day about that," she tells me. "We were talking about who would take Mom and who would take Dad. The reason why it's so important to take care of our parents is actually very simple: They spent a lifetime taking care of us and it becomes our responsibility to take care of them as they grow older. My parents unselfishly made changes in their own lives to better mine, How can I not take care of them?

Although I can never fully repay them for all they have done for me, it would be my pleasure to at least try my best to show my appreciation. The best way I can think of doing so, would be to nuture them, as they nutured me. My siblings and I stand undivided on this topic."

∽

MAI

Children of immigrants often feel like they live in two worlds – the one inside their homes and the one they meet as soon as they walk out the door. Mai is one of those people. (The 24-year-old told me she'd prefer not using her last name because she didn't want her Vietnamese parents to know she was complaining about some of the hardships she endured while growing up.)

Mai knows her parents' lives were hard adjusting to America where they came to be able to freely practice their Catholic religion. She says one of their biggest problems was that they did not speak English or know American customs.

Whenever Mai's relatives would come to her family's home when she was growing up, her relatives would recount their long and frightening boat trip from Vietnam to the United States. "As part of the story, they would tease me," Mai says. "They told me I was in such a hurry to come to the United States that I decided to be born two months early on the boat from Saigon."

After Mai was born, seven more siblings eventually followed. As she got older and more knowledgeable about American culture, Mai says she felt "a sense of duty" to be the family's leader. "There are many pressures on me to this day because everybody expects me to do something for them," she tells me. "I drive my brothers and sisters and parents to the many places they have to go and have been interpreting for my parents since I was 10 years old."

"What kind of interpreting?" I inquire.

"For example, when I go to the doctor's office with my mother and I have to tell the doctor what's bothering her," she explains. "I get so frustrated because my mother yells at me and interrupts the doctor because she wants to know what he is saying."

"Then what do you do?" I ask.

"I tell my mom she has to wait until he's done speaking and then I have to apologize to the doctor for her interrupting," she answers.

Mai also remembers her own struggle to learn English as a little girl. In her home, only Vietnamese was spoken, but when she went to the public school where English was spoken, Mai says she was lost. "I would sit in kindergarten, first, and second grades as quiet as a mouse," she recalls, "and I tried very hard to listen and concentrate because I had trouble understanding the English words. I remember thinking, 'I must be stupid. I'll never learn the language.'"

When Mai tells me she took the bus to and from school every day, I ask her if she ever had any trouble getting to her destinations. She quickly remembers a time when she and her young uncle were returning home from school on the big, yellow bus after their day in kindergarten. "By mistake, we got off at the wrong stop and as the bus pulled away, we both looked at each other with our big, scared eyes, knowing immediately that we had made a mistake and we were lost," she says.

There they were, she vividly remembers, two 5-year-olds who couldn't speak English, with cardboard name and address tags dangling from their little necks. "I cried and told my uncle that I was scared," she says, "then I asked him, 'How are we going to get home?'" She adds that he didn't know, so they slowly started walking down the street, both of them crying at the same time. Then, someone came to their rescue. "A white lady saw us and sensed there was something wrong and she came up to us and asked us some questions in English," Mai recalls. "We just cried and stared blankly at her, so she looked at the cardboard necklaces and walked us home. I didn't understand a word she said, but she talked to us in soothing tones."

Mai tells me it was hard to make friends at school because she couldn't understand English until the third grade. There were years she'd keep to herself on the playground and in the cafeteria, she says. But, as her English improved, so did her ability to make friends.

"Even though I had friends, I would never think of invit-ing them to our home," she says. "I didn't want them to see how our family lived. It was like a prison. There were heavy, black, thick security bars over each win-dow. We were forbidden to play outside after we got home from school because my parents were afraid someone would hurt us."

The small house was crowded, Mai recalls, with its many occupants: her parents, her grandparents, and her siblings. "Each night, I slept in the same queen-sized bed with my four brothers and sisters," she says. "Like sardines, we lay side by side and we filled up all of the spaces from the soft bed's top to its bottom."

And then, Mai tells me something that blows me away because it so much embodies what America means to immigrants and their families. "Even though I was terribly sad about my life," she says, "I remem-ber looking through the bars outside my bedroom win-dow at the bright stars in the sky and thinking to myself, 'One day, I want to be the first female president of the United States.'"

"The first woman president of the United States," I repeat to her and ask, "Do you still have that dream?"

"No," Mai quickly responds. The problem, she says, is that when she dreams her own dreams, she still feels pulled by her family's continued dependence on her. It's as if her look into the future always has the obliga-tions tugging at her. She explains: "Sometimes, I have to help supplement my family's income by delivering newspapers. Ever since I was 8 years old, my father would awaken me early in the morning to help him throw newspapers on the doorsteps of people's homes. I didn't want to get up and work, but I often witnessed my parents' loud arguments over not having enough money to feed the family, so I knew I had no choice but to help, even if it meant delivering papers in the cold and the wet weather."

Mai continues to live in her parents' home, and she's hoping that her bachelor's degree in business education will help her land a job, and maybe one day she'll be able to get her own apartment. But Mai knows that whatever she ends up doing, she'll always need to help her family make their way in the two worlds in which they live.

ᗣᣇ

NATALIA ESTRADA

Natalia Estrada is wearing dark pants and a deep-lime-green cotton shirt with three-quarter-length sleeves and a crisp, pointy collar, and she is talking to me as she approaches. Estrada is apologizing for the hair dye stains on her hands, which I can hardly see.

A 35-year-old hair stylist, Estrada is the mother of three. She greets me with a wide, warm smile, extends her right hand, and says, "I've been looking forward to talking to you."

We order some coffee and sit at a small table in a Sacramento crepe restaurant. Over a whipped-cream-topped iced latte, she answers questions about her childhood. The daughter of Mexican farmworkers, Estrada's excited answers electrify into a series of others as she recounts growing up in California.

She tells me she was 6 months old when her parents crossed the U.S./Mexican border into California illegally, with the help of a "coyote" (smuggler). Her parents, José Baez and Gloria Ramos, were farmworkers, and they brought Estrada and her older siblings José Luis, Miguel, Juan, and Raquel to settle in Santa Paulo, a Southern California agricultural community.

43

Estrada's earliest recollection of the one-bedroom house in which they lived centers on sleeping arrangements. "Mom and Dad slept in the bedroom and all of the kids slept in the living room, and my oldest brother got to sleep on the couch while the others shared two mattresses on the floor," she says. "The girls were raised to clean and cook for everyone and we had to pick up our brothers' clothes. When we came home from school, we had chores to do, so working came first and school came second."

Estrada remembers that her parents were already working in the fields when she and her siblings awoke and got dressed for school. "They worked rain or shine and long hours, too," she says. "They picked lemons, avocados, oranges, grapes, strawberries, and tomatoes, and they turned the dirt with a hoe."

At the end of many days, Estrada remembers her mother boiling salted water for soaking her and Estrada's father's aching, dirty hands. "They would put drops in their eyes for relief from the dirt and sun," she recalls.

Like the other neighborhood's farmworkers' children, Estrada and her siblings struggled to learn English in school because Spanish was the only language spoken at home.

To Estrada, that was the "normal" part of her life.

The memories that are more difficult to recall center on Estrada's father, a man she remembers as being cold and abusive, who favored prostitutes and gambling over his family. She said he loved betting on cards and the fighting roosters he forced his sons to raise in their backyard. "I remember hearing the roosters crowing in the early morning, and on some nights, I saw about 12 men in a circle around the roosters, and I could hear them cheering and cursing," Estrada says. "When everyone was gone, I remember my brother crying and nursing the roosters' wounds with aspirin that my mother had crushed. He loved those roosters!"

Estrada also remembers her mother's black eyes, and the time that she was about 8 years old when some police officers arrived on their front doorstep. "They told my mother that my father might kill her the next time and they gave her the telephone number for Alcoholics Anonymous," Estrada says. "The AA families gave us gifts for Christmas and showed us a different life. There was a lady named Emilia who would invite us over and give us toast with butter and a dash of sugar. Boy, that was the best toast my sister and I ever had!"

Estrada says she and her siblings were glad when her parents split up. Her mother took the children to live with their maternal grandfather in Sacramento. While Estrada's grandfather worked in a soup-packing plant, her mother went back to the fields to pick crops. "I always knew she was a hard worker, but my mother never asked how my day was and I resented it as a child," Estrada recalls.

She also resented being her mother's interpreter. A time Estrada particularly remembers is when she went to the unemployment office with her mother and she had to stand on her tiptoes to talk to the lady behind the counter to ask about applying for unemployment benefits. "The people were rude and treated my mother like she was dumb, and I hate to say it but I did wonder if she was," Estrada says. "They were impatient with us and I blamed my mom."

Estrada remembers yearning to be the child of American-born parents who lived in a pretty house, who did not work in the fields, who had plenty of money, and who would ask about her feelings and how her day went.

Now, Estrada feels guilty for those resentments because as an adult, her view of her mother has a wider lens and comes from a more loving heart. "I didn't get it then. She did everything herself and she taught me that the harder you work for something, the stronger you become," Estrada recalls. "Now, I appreciate where we came from and I have let go of feeling cheated and have become positive."

Estrada is also reminded of a lesson her mother taught her about being proud of her stained hands while paying for food at the grocery store. "I think that's stupid of me to feel like I have to apologize because these are working hands and that's what my mom would say about hers," she says.

Estrada also expresses regret about the way she has raised her own children. She explains that she did not teach them Spanish because she was afraid it would interfere with their ability to learn English in school like it did for her. "It's embarrassing that they do not know Spanish and they don't want to learn it," she laments. "I tell my children to be proud that they are Mexican but I know they are not convinced."

Estrada is trying to lead by example. Now, when she is asked, "What are you?" she no longer answers, "Mexican American." Now she proudly says, "I am Mexican."

She explains, "I am Mexican in my culture and in my blood. I am American because I am here. I am proud of being both. I really am!"

∽

ELISSA PROVANCE

The words "stay hidden, be quiet, and don't make waves" come to mind as I review my interview notes about 51-year-old Elissa Provance, the Communications Director for the Jewish Federation of the Sacramento Region and Managing Editor of its newspaper, *The Jewish Voice*. Provance grew up in New York's Bronx neighborhood, the daughter of a father from Poland and a mother who was born in New York to Polish immigrants.

"I consider myself from peasant stock — very Old World," Provance tells me. "My parents communicated mainly in Yiddish, especially if they didn't want the kids to know what they were talking about."

Provance says that throughout her life, her father's influence has been enormous. She explains that her father, David, was a Holocaust survivor whose entire family murdered. He arrived in the United States in 1950. She says he often told her and her two brothers that America is the greatest country on Earth. "My father wanted nothing to do with his native country," Provance adds. "There was nothing to go back to. I also learned from a very young age to not speak up, to not make waves — just be quiet and everything will be okay. That's how my dad survived - by being quiet and through sheer will. To this day, I struggle with being heard."

Provance says The Bronx was a very mixed neighborhood when she was growing up. Looking back, she realizes she knew a few first- generation children of immigrants from countries including Poland, Hungary, Ireland, China, and several others, but still always felt different. "It was just part of the culture to hear different accents," she recalls, "but not many from Eastern European countries."

Provance says she attended public schools, and her best friend's parents were from Hungary. "The Holocaust was not something we ever talked about," she says. "In fact, it wasn't until a year or so ago that I found out her parents were survivors, just like my Dad."

While growing up, Provance says she saw her father as "a blue- collar guy who wanted to provide for the family." She says he worked several jobs, including being the owner of a restaurant, a Mom- and-Pop candy store, and a card store owner. Her mom worked with her dad for a time, but then went to work as a bookkeeper for several companies in Manhattan, including the construction company that renovated the Statue of Liberty, where her father's name is on the American Immigrant Wall of Honor, a special listing of names of immigrants who came through Ellis Island.

Provance says her father's Holocaust experience has played a key role throughout her life. "While other girls had fantasies about being a ballerina or a bride, I had fantasies about finding one of my Dad's brothers who he believed might still be alive," she recalls. "I felt guilty I could never make it better. He was traumatized by the Holocaust and could not take pleasure in anything. None of us was allowed to experience our own pain because nothing we experienced could ever match what ever happened to my dad. And when something good happened, he managed to sabotage it by picking a fight or teasing us."

Provance says she never wanted to hurt her father's feelings or let him down.

Case in point – when she was in her mid 20s, Provance lived for six months on an Israeli kibbutz. She wanted to live there permanently and become an Israeli citizen, but ended up changing her mind and moving back to the United States. "My Dad made it clear that he would have been devastated without my presence," she explains. "He always had an emotional hold over me."

In addition to honoring her father's wishes, Provance feels responsible for keeping alive his and others' Holocaust experiences. She has served as the chair of the Sacramento region's annual Holocaust commemoration ceremony and was a featured speaker at one of their events. "I don't want my father's experiences to go in vain," she explains. "It's bigger than my dad; it's become the survival of the Jewish people."

Maintaining Jewish traditions has also been important in Provance's life. "I don't want to lose my family's ways, so I cook the same, very traditional dishes my mother did and follow Kosher dietary laws."

Provance adds that food has always played an important role in her life. "It was the source of everything — good times, bad times, and everything in between," she explains.

The mother of two daughters, Provance says she is passing along the traditions to them. "If I don't, it dies in my family and I don't want to take that responsibility," she says.

෬෧

DUTY CALLS

DR. STELLA DARIOTIS

I can't remember when or how the conversation started, but it seems like I've always known that my dentist of 25 years, Dr. Stella Dariotis, is a child of Greek immigrants.

"How are your parents?" I ask each visit, and she usually updates me with a loving and upbeat voice, often with a report that John and Nitsa are either on their way to or have just returned from Greece.

Dr. Dariotis is the elder of two children, was born in Alma, Michigan in 1959, and grew up in Flint, a middle-class American town. She says Flint is where most Greeks lived and it's where her parents owned Bill's Restaurant, a 24-hour operation that featured American fare. "My father partnered with my mom's brother, Bill Kapellas," Dr. Dariotis explains. "They always talked about the restaurant when we had our many family get-togethers and holiday celebrations."

It was at those gatherings where Dr. Dariotis learned about some of her family's history. She says her father had been orphaned at a young age and came to the United States to start a new life when he was 19. Through a mutual friend, her parents met and they both worked at Bill's Restaurant, which had originally been started by Dr. Dariotis' maternal great-grandfather. "When my grandmother, my mom, her sister, and her sister's husband came over from Greece, they went to work right away, even though they didn't know the language," Dr. Dariotis shares. "They worked at the restaurant and lived in the upstairs apartments."

Dr. Dariotis says both of her parents eventually learned English while in America. When they do speak of the past, she says they sometimes talk about their experiences during World War II, when Greece was occupied first by the Italians, and later by the Germans. "My dad has fond memories of the Italians sharing their language and rations with the hungry Greek children, but it was a totally different story with the Germans," she recalls from their stories. "They had very little food and lived in fear, and my mother told me that some people from her village were killed by the Nazis. She also said there were village scouts who were on the lookout for approaching Nazis. They let the village know when the Nazis were coming so they could board up their homes and escape into the mountains."

She says it breaks her heart to think of her beloved parents' suffering during those years.

Dr. Dariotis attended public schools in Flint and she says she felt different from her non-Greek friends. "It always seemed to me that the 'American' kids' lives were simpler," she says. "We immigrant kids had more to deal with, like responsibility and this sense of honor, duty, and obligation to honor family customs and traditions."

That translated into declining some social invitations from her friends, but Dr. Dariotis is quick to point out that she didn't resent it. "We always went to church on Sundays because that was the primary way of maintaining our religious traditions, and it was a very important form of socialization with other Greeks," she explains. "I liked church and as a child, I had looked forward to the holidays and church celebrations and getting together with everyone."

Like her brother George, Dr. Dariotis was required to take lessons in Greek when they were in fourth to sixth grades. "Usually, a woman from Greece would teach us Greek on weekends or a day after school," she says. "It wasn't fun, but there were no ifs, ands, or buts about it; we were going to learn Greek!"

Today, a mother of two sons, Yianni and Marco, Dr. Dariotis carries on the tradition of learning Greek by paying for a tutor for her children. "I feel it is a gift that teaches them who they are and that they are a part of me, my parents' and my grandparents' heritage, and it's a tribute to them," she explains. "It's an integral part of who they are and a connection to family and roots."

She adds that the Greek Orthodox Church and Greek holidays and festivals are also an integral part of her family's life in Sacramento.

Because she is the eldest child, Dr. Dariotis says she has always taken on the responsibility of helping her parents when they've needed it, like completing paperwork for them, making phone calls, or doing some banking. Dr. Dariotis recalls being about 12 and going to the bank to make a deposit for her parents because they didn't know how to do it. "I was a little embarrassed because I thought they should be able to do it, but they insisted it was my obligation to help them," she says. "At times, I've had some resentment even though I know it's been the right thing to do. I've always been responsible and serious; the dependable one."

Dr. Dariotis says her husband, whose grandparents are Italian, tells her she suffers from Greek guilt.

"'Greek guilt'?" I wonder aloud.

"You know," she says, "like 'Go talk to your grand-parents because it makes them so happy.'"

While Dr. Dariotis says she has been expected to help and to be there for family, she also says she has never felt any pressure to marry someone who is Greek or to seek a certain career. However, her parents did tell her that education was important, college was a given, and that the restaurant business was not some-thing she should consider as a career choice because of its round-the-clock demands. "They were always very encouraging and they did tell us we had to have a career, regardless of who we would marry," she recalls. "When we were growing up, my parents would try to take us to Greece every summer and when we got older, they'd send us to Greece for vacations."

Traveling to Greece has become a tradition for Dr. Dariotis' family, too. Her sons have been there twice and will go again for the summer. "Yianni will be attending a camp with some of his close friends in Greece for three weeks and I'm thrilled for him!" she tells me. "My husband and I and Marco are also going there for a family vacation."

Dr. Dariotis says that traveling to Greece has been like opening a book for her. "A book may have a title that gives you insight into what it's about, but it's not until you go into the book when you know what it's about," she says. "It's part of who I am. I am an American of Greek descent; an American first and foremost. But I can't separate the Greek part of me."

෴

NYUIEKO AFUA BANSAH

Texas-born Nyuieko Afua Bansah is 25 years old and she's working and studying hard to make the world a better place. Bansah is currently employed as a health educator for pregnant women while studying for her master's degree in public administration at California State University, East Bay, which is located in Hayward, California. She also dreams of helping poor people in Ghana, but we'll get back to that later in this story.

Bansah was born in Arlington, Texas to parents whose birthplaces circle the globe. Her father, Obed, was born in Ghana, West Africa while her mother, Gartia, was born in Magnolia, Arkansas. (Bansah's parents met through mutual friends in America.) "My father came to the United States in 1976 to attend college after a coup in Romania, which drove many African immigrants out of the country," she explains. "He had been in Romania with a scholarship to study medicine and was supposed to return to work for the Ghanaian government, but the coup changed those plans."

Even though Obed earned a B.A. in sociology from the University of Kansas, he had trouble finding work in his chosen field and ended up working in service-industry jobs, including being a janitor and a taxi driver. Bansah says that after her parents met, they married and moved to Arlington, Texas in search of better jobs.

"Both my parents came from humble beginnings and were the first in their families to attend and graduate from college," she says. "My father eventually earned a master's degree and became a mental health therapist, and my mother also earned a master's degree; hers is in social work."

Throughout her life, Bansah has carried the following message from her parents: "We were always told that excuses are tools for the incompetent," she says. "They said that we could do anything and that everyone has their roadblocks and that you have to get over them. My parents never sugar-coated anything. They had me work at 16 years of age and go to school and it made me more independent and seek knowledge on my own."

The Bansah family eventually looked for better jobs in Visalia, California at the urging of a relative who lived there. "My younger sister and I didn't know when we were young how much they struggled financially, but we did see how hard our parents worked," Bansah tells me. "My parents worked hard and that's why I work hard, too."

Discrimination was at the root of some of her parents' employment difficulties, Bansah tells me. She recalls her father telling her that he didn't know he was "black" until he came to the United States and faced racism when he couldn't get job interviews — even when he was more qualified. "Finding a job and even catching a taxi were difficult for him because not only was he black, but he also had a thick English accent," she explains.

Bansah says she also faced discrimination and name-calling while attending public school in Visalia and later in the Sacramento area, where she moved when she was in fourth grade when her mother found a job as a social worker. She says she got along well with children who were born in the United States, but some of their parents weren't so accepting. She says her friends' parents viewed her negatively, while some fellow classmates took verbal aim at her. "In my early childhood, I was called the occasional 'African Booty Scratcher,' 'Hot Chocolate,' and other terrible names due to my name and people knowing my father was from Africa," she says. "I hid my feelings and didn't hang out with those kids and found people who did accept me, friends who were children of immigrants, themselves."

She adds that as a child, she was embarrassed by her name because it was so different from her class-mates' and because of her father's loud, assertive voice. "His accent was thick and it was hard for my teachers to understand him when he attended my

PTA or teacher/parent conference meetings," she confides.

As she matured, Bansah says her pride about her heritage grew, and she learned to understand the elementary school name-calling, which she says came mostly from African American children. "In college, I took a lot of African study courses, and our teachers opened our eyes to that aspect and it took out the sting," she says. "America doesn't educate people well about people from other countries. I blame it on negative stereotypes created by racism and western imperialism."

Bansah adds that as she got older, she noticed a difference in her peers' attitudes toward her and the world, as well. "I had more African American friends and they became more interested in my experience in being raised in two different cultures," she explains.

As far as any culture clash for her with a father from Africa and a mother from America, Bansah says it has never happened. "I know where I come from and don't want to deny any side," she proudly says. "Both sides fit quite well."

Bansah says that most of her childhood friends were children of immigrants from Ghana, Nigeria, or Brazil. "While in college, I found myself more comfortable with immigrant students and to this day, many of my good friends are immigrants from Africa or the West Indies," she adds.

Bansah says that her understanding of international politics and social development comes from the loud conversations she often overheard while growing up, when her father and his close family friends she calls "uncles" got together. Often, she says, the conversations centered on Ghanaian politics and family ties. Bansah says her father often told stories about the village where he lived with his parents and 12 siblings, and about the political climate in the 1950s. "I remember him talking a lot about Kwame Nkrumah, who was the first president of Ghana, which was the first African country to gain its independence from the British government and become a self-governing republic."

She says they also spoke of government corruption and why it has kept them from returning to their native country.

Bansah says she remembered what those conversations meant when she spent almost two months visiting relatives in Ghana at the age of 13. "Poverty in America has nothing on Third World poverty," she says. "There are handmade houses and food is rationed; water is filthy, and there are no social welfare programs like food stamps. The family unit helps out each other."

Now, as a health educator, Bansah works with women from many different countries, including Mexico, Laos, Nigeria, and some in the Middle East. "I work with them because I feel that the knowledge I give them helps them through their pregnancies and in community life, as well," she explains. "They don't know how our society works and they want to create a better life and not be unemployed and on welfare forever."

As part of her email signature line, Bansah lists the following quote from former South African President Nelson Mandela: "If you talk to a man in a language he understands, that goes to his head. If you talk to him in his language, that goes to his heart."

She says she quotes Mandela because he represents African pride. "African tradition is not about individualism, but rather a collective nature in which we believe every aspect of our lives — including our beliefs, actions, thoughts, and ideas — affects not only us but the people around us," she explains. "Community life and face-to-face interaction are the key to a healthy society."

She is a true believer in helping the poor here and abroad. Her dream one day is to convince the leaders in Ghana to do more for those who are in need. "If you don't do anything for the poor, a country cannot expand socially and economically," she says. "Governments should value the poor."

∽

LEORA AMIR

A friend gave me Leora Amir's phone number, saying she thought she was the daughter of an Israeli immigrant. Amir is 40 years old, was born in Brooklyn, raised in Sacramento, and has always had a curiosity about her parents' past. It turns out that Amir's father, Ezra, was born in Iraq and had fled to Israel for his safety following murderous violence against Jews that began in 1941, when there was a pro-Nazi military coup against the government in Iraq. "I have never heard my father say he was an Iraqi," Amir says. "I've heard him say at times that he's an American who is from Israel."

She says she learned about her father's life in Iraq through stories he told her while she was growing up and through others he related when she asked him more questions during an interview she conducted in 2008. "I remember my dad talking about discrimination, the hard living of being very poor, two of his siblings dying fairly young, how he saw people who were accused of being Israeli spies hanged in public, and the elation of some Muslim Arab witnesses," she shares.

According to Amir, there's another story about some Muslim neighbors who protected her father's family by preventing a Muslim mob from forcing their way into his family's home.

"I saw my dad as a powerful person at a pretty young age because when he was 16, he was in an underground movement," Amir shares. "I am still not sure of all the details but he and others trained together to learn how to use pistols, grenades, Molotov cocktails, and karate to defend themselves and the area in which their families lived in case there were more assaults on the Jews. I know that he and 10 other people secretly left Iraq and walked for six days and nights, led by two Kurdish guides they paid, to cross into Iran and then they took a flight to Cyprus and boarded another to Israel."

Amir says her father's stories have helped her understand him better and to know more about life for Jews in an Arabic country. "I think that as a Jewish person in Iraq, he knew he was never really welcomed there," she says. "The Jews had to be secretive about studying Hebrew and Jewish history, and they were not allowed to travel to Israel/Palestine even though they could openly celebrate holidays together."

Amir tells me her father's family ended up living on an Israeli kibbutz and he met her mother, Marilyn, a native of New York, at work. She told her children that she had traveled to Israel after studying its history, its importance after the Holocaust, and because of a connection she had with a pen pal, who was a Holocaust survivor.

Amir says she felt different from her friends at school growing up in Sacramento, where her family had moved to be closer to her mother's family. The feeling of being different, in part, was related to having Jewish parents who often spoke Hebrew at home and who had memories of experiences from living in different countries. Then, there were the accents – her father's Iraqi-Israeli twist on American words and her mother's intact New York accent. "I felt a little uncomfortable, awkward, and embarrassed at times about my dad's accent, but now I love it and his minor challenges with the English language," Amir recalls. "I remember times when people weren't able to understand my father because of his accent, and there was confusion, but I could always understand him and my mom always made sure to correct his grammar and pronunciation, something he's always welcomed."

But, now, as an adult, Amir says she views it all differently. She refers to her father's odd sentence structures and pronunciations and occasionally funny spelling. Amir provides an example: "I remember once he left a note that said, 'I am going to the jim.' We had had a good laugh about that. My dad thought it was funny, too, after my mom explained to him it's spelled 'gym'."

When Amir was growing up, she says safety was a big issue. "My dad was like a mom because he was overprotective, including cutting out every article about children getting crushed under garage doors," she says. "Safety was a concern on my mother's side of the family, too, due to rampant anti-Semitism in Lithuania before, during, and after World War II and because some of her family members had been mysteriously killed."

Because of safety concerns, Amir's father would take a pen to school permission slips to cross out the parts that he didn't agree with before she could return it for a field trip. "He thought the school should be responsible for me and wouldn't sign something that said they weren't, in case I got hurt," she explains.

Even though she was embarrassed by her father's editing, Amir says her parents taught her important lessons about being safe and standing up for herself and others if ever bullied.

She adds that her parents have also passed along their love of music, dance, art, and Jewish history and culture. "Being Jewish is having intolerance toward injustice and a feeling that a person has an obligation to take action and to speak out about it," she says.

As part of her professional work in education and volunteer efforts, Amir speaks out on behalf of gay rights, and on feminist and disability issues. "Much of my activism has been in front of the Capitol protesting for women's rights and equality, and now in performances that have a message against injustice," she shares. "I have also done some online activism, and have had some door-to-door conversations, too. I think I inherited from my parents the gut feeling that if something is wrong, you should do something about it."

∽

THE ROAD TO SUCCESS

TAMMY MOON

Tammy Moon is 26 years old, an American-born court reporter who is working in Richmond, California, and who is a child of Korean immigrants. Her parents, James and Soung, have each worked for the U.S. Postal Service for more than 25 years, almost as long as they have lived in this country. Moon tells me it was the promise of better economic opportunities that brought her parents to the United States. "To them, and to me, America really is the land of opportunity, where anything and everything is possible," she explains.

Working hard and putting in long hours is what Moon remembers about her parents when she reflects upon her childhood in San Francisco and Sacramento. "I remember my parents leaving for work between 5:00 and 6:00 in the morning when I was in fifth and sixth grade, three hours before I had to leave at 8:00 for school," she says.

To this day, Moon remembers her parents as always being busy, whether at work or at home. "They don't know how to rest," she says. "For example, on my mom's days off, she takes care of my grandpa, getting his food, doing his laundry, paying his bills, taking him to the bank, and in the afternoon, she baby-sits my cousins, and in the evening she goes to a church planning meeting."

Moon recalls that even on the days her mother was sick and went to the doctor, she would go to work instead of staying home to rest. Moon says her parents had the same expectations for her when she was growing up: no excuses and study hard. "I was taught that I had to be half-dead or something very severe to happen to miss school or any activities," she explains. "There were days I could barely even raise my head because I was so weak but still had to go to school because unless you were at a point of physically being unable to move, you were considered to be well enough to go to school."

In addition to attending classes during the day, Moon says she and her sister Julie were expected to attend and excel in after-school activities like tennis, violin, math tutoring, and swimming. "I don't even know why we did so much; it's just what Koreans do, honestly," Moon shares. "They feel that these kinds of extracurriculars are essential to round us as people. We hated it but we had to obey our parents.

"I always felt like I had to perform well in school, which was difficult because I was compared a lot to the other kids," she remembers. "I was under so much pressure to do well, and I never felt like I could accomplish what my parents expected, like getting into Stanford."

Concerning college, expected attendance was always a given. "There was no option not to go to college and nothing was ever said about that," Moon recalls. "We were told the more education we got, the better off we would be — not only financially, but also in terms of status."

When it was time to get a job, Moon says that message was clear, too: "I was taught that you need to work your hardest, no matter the salary, because that's what you've been called to do," Moon explains.

When I ask Moon if there was much emotional expression in her home growing up, she says there was not. "It wasn't because everyone was busy; it had more to do with the Asian culture," she explains. "We never shared emotions growing up; we never hugged or said we loved each other until I was in college."

Because of the lack of emotional expression and being taught not to be confrontational, Moon says that as a child, she learned to keep her feelings inside. As an adult, she's learning to move beyond that. "The most awkward thing has been confronting people when they have done something that has bothered me," she explains, "or listening to things that I've done to others that have bothered them. Through counseling and good friends, I've learned how to confront people and build appropriate boundaries. It sure is a work in progress, though."

If there are any other regrets that Moon has about being a child of immigrants, it's that she wishes her parents would have tried harder to learn to speak English better and to not have lived such an insular life. "I know that their English could have improved exponentially if they had gone to an American church and interacted with American people, because their interaction with Americans was minimal," she adds.

Yet, Moon speaks with admiration for her mother, who eventually took English-as-a-second language (ESL) classes after not being able to sing all of "The Star-Spangled Banner" when she recently visited Disneyland. "Honestly, I didn't know the whole song either," Moon confides, "so when we came back home, she looked up the song so that she could memorize it and rehearse it when she has a chance. That is how she shows she's proud to be an American."

When it comes to celebrating American holidays, Moon says a Korean twist has always been added in her parents' home, making mixing cultures fun. "At Thanksgiving, we always have turkey, cranberries, and mashed potatoes, but we also serve rice, Korean side dishes, Korean soup, and *kalbi* (Korean short ribs)" Moon explains. "The kids will sit at one table and speak and joke in English, while the parents are at the other end of the table, speaking in Korean."

While Moon loves the cultural mix at the holidays, she says her identity is grounded in the American way of life. "I am an American first and a Korean second," she states after I ask if she will have a Korean wedding like her sister Julie had. "I feel that Korea is a part of me, but it isn't a big enough part of me to include that in my wedding. My loyalty and ethic are connected to America, which is my country."

Moon delivers that message loud and clear when people ask her where she's from, a question that is posed by strangers, she says, because of her Asian appearance. "I am adamant in telling people that I am American, and if they want to know more, I tell them I'm American Korean, not Korean American."

∾

JANET RODRIGUEZ

I met 22-year-old Janet Rodriguez at my place of employment in Sacramento. She came to the United States as a teenager and is working during the day and attending college at night.

Rodriguez, pencil-thin and dressed in name-brand clothes, including a stylish shirt, jeans, cropped jacket, and red flats, with her brown hair in a ponytail, proudly mentions that her parents are farmworkers. She stands tall as she talks about how much she admires them and about her early life growing up in Michoacán, Mexico.

In 2001, she came to the United States — Wasco — when she was 15, after her father, José Luis Rodriguez, obtained green cards for him and his wife, Olivia, to work in the fields in California to pick crops. Like her parents and three siblings, Rodriguez spoke only Spanish when she arrived. The children learned English in public schools. "I remember getting picked on by my classmates because they made fun of me for having an accent when I tried to speak English," Rodriguez says. "The saddest part is that some people, including teachers, considered me stupid because I didn't know English."

Rodgriguez remembers the cramped quarters in which her family lived when they first arrived in America. "We stayed in a two-bedroom apartment, and my parents and we four children all slept in the same room. A couple who I didn't know slept in the other room," she says. "We slept on the floor for about four months, until we could afford to buy two beds from a secondhand store."

Rodriguez also remembers her family moving with the harvest so that her parents could work and afford to raise their family. "We moved to a place out in the country to a trailer home where my dad didn't pay rent, and I hated it there," she recalls. "On occasion, I could hear my dad's supervisor yelling at him, insulting him with bad language, and when I asked my dad why he allowed it, he would simply say, 'That's how things work. I can't complain because I don't pay rent.'"

Rodriguez helps me picture what she calls an "ordinary day" during the years she lived with her parents in Wasco and she attended college classes: Her alarm clock registers 3:45 in the morning, and the light from her parents' room awakens her. It is her mother's time to get ready to go pick grapes in the fields. Rodriguez tries to go back to sleep, but she cannot, and she turns on her side to see her two little sisters, Rosario and Johanna (ages 12 and 9 at the time), who share her bed and are fast asleep. When Rodriguez's mother opens the girls' bedroom door to check on them, like she does every morning, Rodriguez closes her eyes and pretends to be asleep so her mother won't feel bad that she has awakened her during her morning ritual. "She stands there for a brief minute and I wonder what she is thinking," Rodriguez says about a particular morning she recalls.

Rodriguez knows that her mother picks grapes nine hours a day, six days a week, and is paid $6.75 an hour.

She also knows that her parents are lucky if they get to see each other for 20 minutes a day, because they work different shifts in order to take care of their family, which has grown to six children.

Rodriguez adds that her father works in the fields overnight for 13 hours. "He leaves home at 4:00 p.m. after he cooks something for my little sisters, who come home from school, and he tries to keep the house clean," she says.

Rodriguez says she appreciates the fact that her father's doing house chores is not a common occurrence. "He doesn't care what our Mexican culture says," she explains. "In our culture, women have been taught to do chores and look pretty so they could find husbands, while men haven't been expected to do any house chores because they are the breadwinners."

With parents as farmworkers, Rodriguez's child-hood memories in the United States are directly related to the fields, even though she has never worked in them.

"It is depressing to look at my father's red and irritated eyes that he gets from pesticides in the fields and from his lack of sleep," she says. "He always washed his clothes separately from ours because of the chemicals, and he wouldn't let us hug him until after he took a shower."

Rodriguez also remembers a time when her mother came back from working in the fields on a 110-degree day, her face burned and lined from long days in the searing sun. "My mom put her dirt-covered lunch bag on the ground and carefully removed a bandana from her head, revealing her messy, dirty hair, and she still looked beautiful to me," Rodriguez recalls. "My friend was with me, and I wanted to show my mom how proud I was of her and tried to hug her but she moved away. I remember her telling me that she smelled bad because of the sweat and dirt and I told her I didn't care and gave her a big hug and kissed her sweaty cheeks."

While Rodriguez appreciates her parents' hard work, she does not miss the irony that she lives in quite a different world. "Because my parents toil and sweat in the fields every day, my two older brothers, Luis and Victor, and I are now able to attend college," Rodriguez says. "Unlike my parents, when I get up in the morning, I dress nicely for school, have time to eat a good breakfast, drive to school, and sit in an air-conditioned classroom. Sometimes, on my way to school, I imagine my parents wiping the sweat and dirt from their faces while working in a blistering, hot grape field. The only sweat I wipe off my face is during my soccer games and exercise routines."

Attending college was not an easy sell for Rodriguez back in 2004, when she graduated from Wasco High School with a 4.0 average. "Although one of the reasons my parents came to this country was for their children to receive an education, it didn't necessarily mean they wanted their boys and their girls to go on to college," Rodriguez explains. "They thought that because I was a female, I could find a guy to take care of me and have children and forget all about my career, while my brothers needed to get an education because they would be able to provide a good future for their children."

Rodriguez was able to change her parents' minds after many conversations and many talks with them and because of her ability to get financial aid to pay for her tuition. "Today, they are my greatest supporters for me to continue my education and they encourage my younger sisters to excel academically," Rodriguez says.

In addition to serving as a role model for her younger sisters, Rodriguez also works with other Latinas, including serving as a counselor for students of migrant workers, for whom she provides tutoring and college financial aid counseling. "One of my most important aspirations is to make Latinas realize their scholastic potential," she says.

Each day, Rodriguez carries with her a promise to herself and her family that she will demonstrate that all of her parents' sacrifices and hard work have not been in vain. She recently graduated with honors from California State University, Sacramento, with a degree in intercultural communication, and is continuing graduate studies toward a master's in social and political communication. She is also awaiting word about a full-time job with benefits that she is hoping to get any day now.

∽

JAHAN HERAVI

Twenty-three-year-old Jahan Heravi*, who was born in Kabul, Afghanistan, tells me that she had a hard time assimilating in the United States after arriving here in 2001 at the age of 14. She left behind a war-torn country and brought with her horrific memories of a missile hitting her home, and the family crouching in the bathroom as more missiles landed in their backyard. Heravi was four years old at the time. "In that bathroom, praying for our dear lives, my parents decided to leave our home and emigrate to Pakistan," Heravi states. "However, the border between the two countries was closed, so we had to live in various camps in extremely grotesque conditions, with no food or water. When we did make the journey to Peshawar, Pakistan, I was scared because there were checkpoints and the Taliban asked our driver where we were going and why."

Before the Taliban took control in Afghanistan, Heravi tells me her mother held a prominent position as a judge, and her father was a veterinarian. She says her mother also was a director of a school for girls and a leader of a nonprofit organization to help illiterate women earn a living by making crafts. "After the Taliban was in charge, they made all the women stay home and do nothing," Heravi tells me. "My mother had girls come to our home instead of school and when the Taliban found out, she had to shut down the underground school."

Because of fear for their safety, Heravi says her parents, brother, and sister moved back and forth between Afghanistan and Pakistan several times before emigrating to the United States.

First came Heravi's mother, who had asked for political asylum after she had come to the United States to speak about her work in Afghanistan. "It was really hard to be separated from her, especially because I am the youngest and I was attached to my mom," Heravi recalls. "She would call us every now and then to check on us, and she comforted me by saying that she would make arrangements for us to join her."

In June of 2001, Heravi's father, sister, and brother moved to Fremont, California, where her mother and maternal uncle lived. "I was scared to move again," she recalls. "Whenever I tried to adjust to one place, we had to move to another. I had to change schools and to leave new friends and go to another country. The United States was completely different from what I was used to and I had only known entry-level English."

In September of 2001, Heravi started public high school as a freshman. Immediately, her family's cultural traditions and values were in conflict with what was considered "normal" in America. "I wasn't used to being around boys or talking to boys since I used to go to all-girls schools," she explains. "After coming here, it was hard since we shared the same classrooms and we had to participate in group projects."

Heravi says she gained a reputation for being shy because she was quiet in class. Her fellow classmates didn't know there were good reasons for her silence. She says it was because she had been afraid that people would laugh at her accent. She says what she feared more was that her classmates would learn that she really wasn't the person she pretended to be.

Less than two weeks after Heravi started school, terrorists attacked the United States by flying airplanes into prominent buildings, and murdered about 3,000 people, most of them Americans. At the time, Heravi had been assigned to ESL classes because of her rudi-mentary English. There's where she received and took some advice from her ESL teacher. "I remember the day the teachers were talking about the attack, but I didn't even understand what they were talking about and didn't know the intensity of the attack until I went home and was told by my parents," she says. "The next day, I went to school and my ESL teacher told me and my siblings not to tell anyone that we were from Afghanistan because she was afraid the teenagers might cause harm to us. So, we had to tell my friends, most of whom were Indian and Asian children of immigrants, that we were from India."

Heravi says she and her siblings spoke Hindi, but it was hard to keep up the Indian front, especially because she had never been to India. "I always felt a sense of guilt for lying to my friends, but I was scared about what people might do to me and I didn't know what to do," she explains. "It wasn't until my family decided to move to Roseville, California and I had to change high schools that I told them the truth, and they were very sympathetic."

By the time Heravi had graduated from high school, she had excelled in her class subjects thanks to her doggedness at learning English by attending classes during and after school. "In my life, education has been precious and has often come with great costs, so I was determined to take advantage of my education opportunities," Heravi shares.

Ever since her junior year in high school, Heravi has worked to support her family because of financial hardship. She says her siblings have helped, too. "Even in choosing colleges, I was unable to attend better universities that were farther away because of my obligations to my family," she says without complaining. "I am accepting," she says. "When my parents could, they supported us and raised us and if they cannot, then it's up to the kids to support them."

Heravi explains that her parents had previously worked for computer companies in Fremont, and moved to Roseville where they could better afford a bigger house. She adds that financial problems arose when a cigarette store they owned did not make enough profit and they were forced to sell it.

Today, Heravi lives with her parents, her sister, and her brother. She says living together and supporting each other are among the ways her family honors its culture.

They also work together for a common goal – to become U.S. citizens. "At the end of December we applied," she tells me. "We practice together and we encourage my dad as we prepare for our tests."

A recent college graduate with a degree in criminal justice, Heravi is in the process of applying to law school. She tells me her selection to the Judicial Internship Program of Sacramento Superior Court has changed her life. She says it happened when she was participating in a courtroom mock trial and had the opportunity to act as a defense attorney representing an indigent client.

In a personal statement for a law school admission application, Heravi wrote:

The most valuable feature I cherish in the United States is that this is truly the land of opportunities – a land where I hope to be a public defender, to help the underserved who are plagued by systematic social, racial, and economic problems, just as I had been haunted by similar conflicts but in a different context. That is the beauty of this country, that someone like me, who was born in Afghanistan, barely escaped the atrocities of war, lived in a refugee camp, attended six elementary schools (including an underground school), and immigrated four times to another country, can now dream of standing before a judge to represent those who have faced adversity and call that courtroom home.

———

*Jahan asked that a different last name be used because of safety concerns.

∾

MADELYN ESTRADA

"You have to talk to Madelyn Estrada," my friend Jack Katz, said when he learned about this book. "She is our former nanny's daughter and a real success story."

By success, Jack is referring to Estrada's current quest for her master's degree in applied economics from Johns Hopkins University in Baltimore, Maryland. It's been quite a path that this 27-year-old woman has traveled to get from a developing nation to an American working-class neighborhood, and now to a prestigious university.

Estrada arrived in Rockville, Maryland from Guatemala when she was 7 years old. She, her sisters Rocio and Emmy, and her father, Luis Eduardo, came to the United States to join her mother, Mariana, who had arrived two years earlier to work as a nanny. "My mother came to the United States when she and my father were going through a rough patch in their marriage," Estrada explains. "My mother's older sister was working as a nanny in Maryland at the time and persuaded her to come to the states with the promise that she would help my mother find full-time employment."

The promise was kept and Estrada's mother worked for my friends Jack and Lynn in Chevy Chase, Maryland where she was a nanny for their little girl.

By the time Estrada's parents had patched up their marriage and the family all lived under one roof again, the job hunt for her father became grueling. While in Guatemala, Estrada's father had a good job and benefits, thanks to his work for a tire-manufacturing company, but in the United States, he was a day laborer. Estrada remembers seeing him outside a 7-Eleven store, desperately looking at the cars that pulled up, hoping that someone would hire him to work. Her vantage point was a public transit bus that she and her sisters were riding to go to Chevy Chase to join their mother at her job. "Here we were going to a rich kid's house to play and there was my dad with his chapped lips and his face burned and red from being in the sun, waiting for work," she says. "It was heart-breaking, but he always eased our pain because he told us that it was his honor to provide for his family. His sense of honor rose over the fact that people would mock him because he did not speak English well, and he never mentioned the calluses, blisters, and scars we noticed on his hands from the manual labor he did."

Estrada remembers her father telling her to expect to work hard for the things she wanted to achieve in life, and to remember, "If you don't break a sweat doing it, it probably isn't really worth it." She says her dad's words, ethics, integrity, and sacrifices have often helped her cope when school and life have proved difficult. She says they have also motivated her to make positive choices in her life, including when she was in high school and had many temptations to do the opposite of what she was supposed to do, like skipping classes and going to parties.

While her father was looked down upon by some Americans, Estrada says her mother and sisters experienced much more acceptance in Chevy Chase, Maryland than they did in Rockville. "It was a very positive experience for us because most people had nannies in that community, and we were never looked upon as being children of 'the help'," she says. "Jack and Lynn were always so nice to us and during summer vacations, we got to go to the zoo and museums with their daughter, Melissa. In some ways, it felt like we grew up in Chevy Chase a little bit."

The acceptance in Chevy Chase was a confidence-builder and a relief for Estrada, who said public school in Rockville was a different story. "Elementary school was super tough for me," Estrada says. "We were the newest immigrants in our community and so the kids at school did not want to associate with us. I was teased because I could not speak English, even by some kids who were also children of immigrants."

Estrada specifically remembers speaking Spanish to a classmate from Nicaragua. "She looked like me and when I spoke to her in Spanish, a language I know she knew, she answered back in English. I was so confused and humiliated!" she remembers. "I was trying to overcome the language barrier, was teased for being chubby and wearing hand-me-down clothes, and had to sit by myself in the cafeteria."

Even though she was miserable in elementary school, Estrada told her parents that everything was just fine. "There was so much going on at home and my little sister hated day care, so I figured I could bring at least one bit of good news a day and I did," she says. "I felt like I had to protect my parents and I decided that while I was the chubby one and didn't have as many talents or smarts as my sisters, I could be the one to make people smile, so being happy was my role."

Middle school was a bit easier, Estrada says, because most of her friends were from Central America and she could fit in better by changing into baggy clothes in the school bathroom to look like the other kids.

Socializing after school was forbidden in the Estrada household. "My parents started work early and by the time we got home from school, we were not allowed to leave the house," she says. "My older sister was in charge and she was like a second mom to us. We lived in our own little world where we would play with Barbie dolls and no one would judge us."

Estrada says her parents were overprotective throughout her school years and it proved to be embarrassing. "They would walk us to the bus stop when we were young and would not leave until the bus was out of sight," she explains. "We were not allowed to go to school dances, sleepovers, and all activities that are an integral part of the school culture," she explains. "Most kids looked at us like it was a foreigner thing and they thought it was quite strange, especially when we got to high school. I resented that my parents were not being 'cool' parents."

Estrada says her mother, a devout Catholic, often told her and her sisters about the importance of saving sex for marriage. "It was overbearing at times because she had this conversation with us every time before we went to a youth group or church dance," Estrada says. "My mother was always at the events being a chaperone, and she used every opportunity to remind us that while we may fall in love, it would inhibit our growth if we strayed from our religious values. She was a religious woman and a conservative feminist, teaching us to value ourselves and to take advantage of educational opportunities so that we would never have to depend only on men."

When Estrada went to St. Mary's College in South Bend, Indiana, it was the first time she had been away from her tight-knight family. She joined her sister Rocio, who had already been at the school for a year. "We were two of five Latina women on St. Mary's campus and people wanted to know more about us in a positive way," she says. "It was finally a cool thing to be foreigners."

Estrada says it was the acceptance on her college campus that helped her feel more comfortable about being an immigrant. She adds that the popularity of singer Jennifer Lopez also helped. "Jennifer Lopez was really 'in' so everyone thought it was cool to look different," she says.

"Before college, I felt a huge difference from native-born Americans, but going away to college really closed the gap," she reflects. "Being part of an educated demographic has put us all on a similar playing field.

"Then, when we gained our citizenship and our Latina friends were so happy for us because it was a big deal, we began to see it as a big deal ourselves," Estrada recalls. "We were actually official."

Being official was an important source of pride and security for the Estrada family. Prior to that, her mother had sent in paperwork to the State Department to extend their visas, which had expired, and there was constant fear of government raids that might lead to deportation. "With our citizenship, we became part of this special club in the United States," she says. "This country has an all-star team and our citizenship helps us blend in, and we earned the right to be called Americans just like everyone else."

From the first day she arrived in the United States, Estrada says her mother told her she could be anything she wanted to be. That message was reinforced by her father and her mother's employers who both often asked her what she wanted to be when she grew up. "At first, I wanted to be a ballerina and then I was inspired by all of the art history books in Jack and Lynn's house and I wanted to become an artist," she recalls. "I always had a soft spot for wanting to be a lawyer like Jack and Lynn because they were all of the glory of the 'American dream,' and I wanted to be like them when I grew up."

The importance of an education was repeated at school, at her mother's employers' home, and by Estrada's parents. "My mother gave us the courage to dream big," Estrada shares. "I was told I had to help her with the cleaning and she reminded me that if I did not do well in school, cleaning homes would be my future career."

"My parents often said that they will probably not bequest us with anything of real tangible worth, except a formal education," she says. "My parents' famous words were, 'The only thing that they couldn't take away from you is your education...we came to this country to progress, so you have to be better than us.' To this day, my parents have very accented English; however, they are independent and self-sufficient and they never really depended on us to translate for them."

Estrada says she is very proud of her Mayan heritage and goes back to Guatemala when time and money allow. "I like to remind myself of who I am and where I come from," she says. "I am proud to be an American, but I am not completely at home here. I feel more Guatemalan, and like my parents, I get homesick for Guatemala's close-knit neighborhoods and extended family gatherings and carnivals."

Today, Estrada is a full-time graduate student. She is married to Mauricio Giron, who is a child of immigrants from El Salvador and works as a certified public accountant for one of the big four accounting firms. "Even though Mauricio and I come from Latin America, we view ourselves differently because he was born in the United States," she says. "He identifies as being Latino American first and then the child of Salvadorian immigrants."

At the time of this interview, Estrada has been married for three years, and she was looking forward to a future filled with several dreams, including a full-time job, a PhD in economics, helping parents and in-laws to retire, and having children. "We want our kids to have even more options than we did growing up," she says.

∽

ON THE OUTSIDE

HANI AHMAD

It's been many years since I've had contact with my high school and college boyfriend, Hani Ahmad, a Palestinian American. This book led me back to him via a mutual friend, and his answers to my questions were more surprising than I had anticipated. Even though we were "together" for approximately six years during high school and college, I knew so little of the prejudice he and his family have endured. When we were teenagers, I had heard from his parents that they were not welcomed when they moved to a small home in Forty Fort, Pennsylvania, in the late 1940's. However, that was the only mention they made during the years that I had known them.

Ahmad's mother, Qudsia, and his father, Hassan, had always welcomed me into their home. I felt loved and accepted there, and we didn't dwell on religion — my Jewish faith and their Muslim faith were private matters. Instead, we shared wonderful times together around their dinner table, eating luscious food like babganoush, stuffed grape leaves, and kibbe, and we regularly watched television together in their family room, with beautiful, red Ooriental rugs underneath our feet. The atmosphere in the Ahmad home was one of acceptance and calmness whenever I was there, except for some occasional physical jousting between four brothers.

Ahmad's memories about growing up in Forty Fort are filled with conflicting emotions. He has both love and admiration for his parents, but when he looks back at his youth, he remembers feeling uncomfortable about his Arabic heritage.

"I knew a little bit of Arabic when I was about 3 or 4," he remembers, "and when I was playing in the neighborhood and my mom would call me in Arabic, the kids would tease me. So, I always made sure to answer her back in English."

He adds that he had a strong desire to fit in more easily with the mostly Caucasian, Christian community around him and had been aware of the negative images of Arabs in the media. Because Ahmad's skin was somewhat lighter than his brothers', he was often mistaken for having a Mediterranean or Latin background and never offered a correction. He would say something like, "I'm a pretty eclectic mix," and leave it at that.

Now, he says, at the age of 57, he feels guilty talking about his distancing attitudes and adds with a heavy voice, "Things were the way they were. There were reasons."

Today, Ahmad is a Licensed Clinical Social Worker employed in private practice in Colorado Springs, and is a part-time counselor at Colorado College. He participates in a college group of first-generation college students, many of whom are first-generation citizens and represent ethnic and racial minorities. "We talk about what it is to be a minority," he says. "Maybe I can help them not be embarrassed and not to be sad and guilty for how they may have treated their parents."

Like his mother, Ahmad writes letters to the editor about Middle East/Palestinian issues and has seen some published in newspapers, like the *New York Times*. "My parents tried to make sure I understood the difference between the policies of the government and the hearts and minds of people," he says.

Ahmad's father had come to the United States as a teenager to start a new life after growing up as a sheepherder in what is now the West Bank. He returned to Palestine 25 years later and married Qudsia, a college-educated woman, among the first female broadcasters in Jerusalem, and the daughter of a Palestinian diplomat. They had planned to stay in Jerusalem, but in 1947, they decided to leave during the outbreak of violence during the fight for Israeli independence. "My mother's father agreed that it was best for my parents to leave their families in Palestine and move to the United States, where my father was already a citizen," Ahmad explains.

Over the years, Ahmad has heard stories from his parents and brothers about discrimination in the United States. The earliest was when they moved into a home on what appeared to be a quiet, a tree-lined street in Forty Fort. One story recalls the time when someone shot at windows in the Ahmad home; another focuses on one neighbor who moved out when the Ahmads refused to leave; and yet several others involve name-calling by neighbors against family members. One specific incident happened in a nearby public park. As Ahmad tells, it, his mother was there with her four young sons and a stranger told her she couldn't sit on the park bench because of the color of her skin. He said that she defensively explained that it was a public bench and yet, she left out of embarrassment and in fear for her and her children's safety.

Ahmad remembers his own discrimination as a child. He mentions a backyard neighbor who denied access to his property to the four brothers as a shortcut to a mall and a main street — something he would afford to other neighborhood children. "He would shout at us and say, 'Get out. You can't go on my property. Why don't you go back to Puerto Rico?'"

Ahmad recalls that most of his fellow school students were accepting, but he does remember being taunted with a few words like "nigger" and "camel jockey" because while people noticed his skin was darker than others, they didn't know which prejudice was the "correctly" targeted one. "The name- calling made me feel alien and angry," he says.

Some teachers didn't help, either. Ahmad remembers one winter when he was in fourth grade and his public school teacher singled him out to answer the question about where Jesus was born. He stood to attention, as required, with his heart racing and fear building, only to see the many hands waving in the air, awaiting recognition and the opportunity to respond. "Humiliated, I was about to say that I didn't know the answer," he says, "but then I remembered the line from a Christmas carol, 'Christ was born in Bethlehem'. I'm quite sure the teacher had called on me because she suspected that I didn't know the answer."

While his parents were Muslims and introduced their four sons to the faith, only the oldest, Dean, embraced it. "They taught us prayers at meal time, but I did not grow up with a connection to religion," Ahmad explains. "I remember my mom saying I would have to decide which religion, if any, I wanted to practice. ... There was no mosque or Arabic community where we grew up."

Because they did not have an Arabic/Muslim community of their own, Ahmad thinks that he and his brothers unconsciously gravitated toward other minorities, including toward those of the Jewish faith. His brothers had good friends who were Jewish and one of his brothers, Malek, married a Jewish woman. It was all perfectly fine with his parents, he says, because they practiced and taught tolerance.

Ahmad shares another story he has heard about his mother joining forces with two Jewish mothers when a high school history teacher said that those who practiced a non-Christian religion meant that they were pagans. "They all got together and went to school and said, 'What the hell is this?'" Ahmad relates.

Ahmad says his parents made a point of repeatedly telling their four sons to not to let bigotry or racism get in their way of working hard, excelling academically, and achieving success. He says they also told their sons to exercise caution: "They believed the U.S. government and its people were generally ignorant and/or biased against Arabs, in general, and especially Palestinians, who were seen as recalcitrant in their objections to Zionism and the establishment and expansion of Israel."

Ahmad says he imparts his parents' lessons to his own children, Zachary and Marlee. "I tell my children to work against bigotry and use every opportunity to promote understanding and justice. ... one of my father's favorite sayings was, 'There's your side of the story...There's my side of the story, and then there's the truth.'"

As far as his own identity, Ahmad says he sees himself as a Palestinian American. He adds that because of his name, people view him in a different light than they do others. His example: "Say I'm talking to someone at a hardware store and the person doesn't know if I'm Greek or Italian. I pull out my credit card they see the name, Ahmad, and his whole demeanor changes. At first, we were joking, and after he saw my ID, the whole conversation changes. I can see it in his face and friendliness. The prejudice still exists."

Ahmad says his children have fought against unfair treatment, as well, and they have been cautious. On September 11, 2001, when al-Qaieda terrorists attacked the United States, Ahmad says it was tough for his children on several levels — as Americans who denounced the attacks, and as children of an Arabic parent. "I remember my son saying to my daughter, 'Don't take any shit from anybody,'" he shares.

Like his parents, Ahmad and his family appreciate living in the United States and are proud to be Americans.. He explains, "I'll take America, warts and all, and vociferously argue for even more freedom and justice in both domestic and foreign affairs. My parents were right about this being an imperfect country, but it is the best in terms of opportunities and personal freedoms."

Postscript: Ahmad urged me to contact one of his older brothers, Maher, for some of his reminiscences because he wanted to make sure they were accurate. Maher lives in Los Angeles. He is a production designer for feature films and is responsible for the scenery and the sets in popular films including *Gangster Squad, Dodgeball* and *Zombieland*.

Our contact is made several months after Qudsia's passing, and many of Maher's memories center around her. He remembers his mother defending him and his brothers from neighborhood taunts and from prejudice by school teachers. "She was not shy about taking up matters about the faculty with the principal and the school board," he recalls.

He also recalls a young teenager in the neighborhood who would cut down the family's clothes from the backyard clothesline where his mother had them hanging to dry. Maher tells me the teenager once threw a large, dead fish against their house, and that it was not unusual for him to knock on their doors and windows at night to frighten the family inside.

He remembers a summer job during his middle-school years when he worked on a farm along the Susquehanna River. "I picked corn and tomatoes and I remember a guy taking my face in his hands and saying directly to me, 'It's good to have a nigger working for me.'"

Maher says he continued working at the farm after the incident because, at the time, he did not realize then how ridiculously insulting those words were." "I didn't have the cognitive maturity at that time to process what the insult was," he reflects.

Maher's reminiscences also include accompanying his mother (when he was about 9 years old) to church gatherings where she had been invited to speak about the Muslim faith. He also recalls Christmas trees and Easter baskets in his home at Christmas and Easter times. "They had no problem with us enjoying Christmas and Easter as long as we were interested," he says.

When Maher was in grade school, he remembers the Protestant children (the majority of the school population) being dismissed at 2:00 p.m. to go to religious instruction. "That left me and the Jewish kids at school for another hour," Maher says. "I have always identified with Jews and most of my friends have been Jewish."

While a student at Northwestern University, Maher became an activist (like his mother) for Palestinian rights, and also for gay rights. "I am a member of two minority groups," Maher tells me. "There are three identifiers of who I am. I am an American. I am a Palestinian, and I am a gay person...There were years when I had a burning sense of injustice that needed to be rectified, combined with my belief (that maybe was foolish) that you could speak to people and make a difference."

Maher sends me an article that he had published in the *Chicago Tribune* in 1981 in which he talks about Palestinian rights, Zionism, the politics of the Middle East, and the hope for peace. "Since that article was written, so little has changed in the Middle East," he says sadly. "It's really depressing."

∽

DR. JOE TURNER

When Dr. Joe Turner moved to Youngstown, Ohio from Haifa, Israel at the age of 10, he wasn't very happy about it. He tells me that it wasn't easy leaving behind a country and people he loved so much. "I had a happy childhood in Israel after moving there from Brazil when I was 5," he says

Dr. Turner is a 59-year-old ear, nose, and throat surgeon in Pittsburgh, Pennsylvania and he adds, "Israel was a young kids' country when I was there, and I remember my friends and I taking buses in Haifa. Public transportation was great and we could go anywhere we wanted. I didn't particularly like the idea of going to the United States."

Moving was his parents' idea. His father, Rafael, also a medical doctor, wanted to open his own private practice and couldn't do it in Israel. "My father's hours and pay were fixed by the socialized medical system in Israel," Dr. Turner explains. "My dad had to start all over in America, even though he had been trained at the Illinois Eye and Ear Infirmary in the 1940s," Dr. Turner explains. "When he had been offered several internship opportunities at hospitals, he chose Youngstown."

While his father was interning at Northside Hospital, Dr. Turner was entering sixth grade. The problem was that while he knew how to speak Hebrew and he understood Portuguese, it wasn't of any help in the classroom. "I was always good in math but could not read or write English well," he says. "It was like going to school in the dark."

Dr. Turner says his father hired a tutor, but English wasn't an easy language for him to master quickly. "It wasn't fun or pleasant because you were going to school and not understanding very much," he remembers. "And when you have a language barrier, it's hard to be buddies with anybody. I felt like an outsider."

Dr. Turner says it wasn't until the 10th grade that he felt like he had a command of the English language and looking back, he says he has no idea how he passed his classes along the way.

He adds that what also helped in 10th grade was having an understanding of American sports and teenage culture.

As another part of his assimilation, Dr. Turner followed his older brother's lead and changed his birth last name of Tarnopolsky to Turner. "It wasn't because of discrimination," he explains. "It was because it was too hard for people in America to pronounce my name, and changing it made life easier."

What also made Dr. Turner feel more at ease was belonging to the Jewish Community Center in

Youngstown. "My language problems were not as uncomfortable there, and most of my friends ended up being from the Jewish side of town," he says.

Dr. Turner says his parents never expected him to become a physician, but his father always emphasized the importance of a good education. "My dad always said to go to school so that you could do well anywhere," he remembers.

It was when he was a sophomore at Miami University in Oxford, Ohio that Dr. Turner says he decided to become a doctor. While a medical student at The Ohio State University School of Medicine, Dr. Turner returned to his beloved Israel and received training for a couple of months in Jerusalem, where he worked at a Hadassah hospital.

After graduation, Dr. Turner moved to Pittsburgh for an internship at the Eye and Ear Infirmary. He has been in practice there for 30 years. Married for 30 years to his wife, Marilyn, whom he met in Pittsburgh, Dr. Turner is the father of three children, all of whom attended Jewish schools when they were young.

"In retrospect, are you glad your parents brought you to the United States?" I ask.

"I have a good life here," he immediately responds. "I think I would have had a good life in Israel and Brazil. At times, I would think about what life would be like if we were not in the United States, and I have thought maybe I would have been a war casualty in Israel."

As we end our interview, I learn that Dr. Turner, Marilyn, and his father, Dr. Tarnopolsky, are planning a trip to Israel to visit family, for some sightseeing, and "to reconnect."

I ask Dr. Turner, "If someone were to ask you, 'How do you identify yourself?' would you say you are an American, a Brazilian American, or an Israeli American?"

"I would say I am a Jewish American," he responds.

෴

MIKE MENDOZA

Mike Mendoza, a handsome and fit personal trainer in Sacramento, says one of the most vivid memories he has of growing up in Concord, California, is when the telephone would ring in the house he shared with his father, Pedro, mother, Erlinda, and siblings, Melissa and Charles. He remembers racing to answer the phone because he was petrified that his parents might arrive first. He knew that once his parents' Tagalog-accented voices were heard by his friends, it would be the perfect opportunity for them to use it as ammunition to tease him. "I can't understand what your parents are saying," Mendoza recalls his friends' mocking voices. "Then they'd repeat what my parents said and make fun of them."

He tells me he would react with a laugh, as if their teasing didn't matter, but it did. Even though the taunts bothered him, Mendoza adds that he didn't challenge his friends. He says that all he was focused on was trying to fit in with his Caucasian buddies. Mendoza was the only Filipino in his group of friends, he explains, and the last thing he wanted was to be viewed differently by his peers. "I grew up feeling painfully different than other children because of the color of my skin, the way my parents spoke, as well as the food I ate at my home," the 28-year-old says.

So, when Mendoza's friends came over to his house to hang out when he was a child, Mendoza made sure to steer them away from the sights inside and instead, get out to the backyard as soon as possible. "I was always trying to direct them outside because I didn't want them to see anything that they could use to tease me," he says. "We had a lot of Filipino décor in our house, like pictures on the wall with a map of the country or a beach in Manila, and lots of traditionally dressed dolls from the Philippines."

If lunch was in the plans, Mendoza says he'd ask his father to make hamburgers and hot dogs and not to serve anything "ethnic" like lumpia, a popular Filipino dish much like eggrolls, or pansit, a favorite noodle dish in his parents' native country.

That fear of being teased also motivated Mendoza to keep his friends away from the religious altar his devoutly Catholic parents had erected in the home. He says it was located in a living room corner and was made of oak-colored wood and featured a large cross with a life-sized picture of Jesus that was surrounded by smaller pictures of the Virgin Mary and small vials of Holy Water. "I was petrified that my friends would see that," Mendoza remembers, "because my friends' homes had nothing like that."

If Mendoza had his druthers, he says he would have played at his friends' houses all of the time. "Whenever I would go to their houses, I would study how they did things, the kind of food they ate, and I would want to live like they lived because I thought that was 'normal,'" he says.

Mendoza remembers being asked often about his ethnicity. "What are you?" he says, was a common question. "Once when I was about 8, and an older woman asked that question and I told her I was Filipino, she responded, 'Oh, I've never seen one of you.' It made me feel like she viewed me as a dog and wanted to know what breed I was."

Defining who he was to himself was confusing, Mendoza says. "I felt like I was not completely Filipino because I couldn't speak the language, and I wasn't American because of the way I looked," he recalls. "I always felt like I was somewhere in between and that was a very lonely feeling because I felt like the only one back then, like I couldn't really relate to anyone."

Mendoza's parents, who came to this country to earn graduate degrees in 1964, always instilled in Mendoza and his siblings the importance of education to elevate them in American society and to help them in their job searches. "My father is very intelligent and was valedictorian of his high school," Mendoza boasts. "He majored in chemistry in college and earned a master's degree in botany, while my mother became a pharmacist."

Mendoza adds that his father set an example of working hard in spite of adversity. "He was one of eight children and was born without some of his fingers and toes, so he had to work hard to prove his capabilities as a chemist," Mendoza adds. "He speaks the most often of missing the Philippines, but both of my parents keep in close contact with their families."

When friends or relatives come over to visit his parents' household and speak Tagalog with them, Mendoza says it makes him regretful that he had not been taught the language. "My roommate in college was Filipino and when he spoke with my father, there was such a comfortable feeling between them," he says. "I can understand many of the words that they share, but I can't speak the language well."

While this story is being written, Mendoza is in the midst of preparing to marry Tiffany, his girlfriend of four years. He has decided that even though Tiffany is Caucasian, he wants to recognize his Filipino roots in the wedding ceremony because he believes it is time to embrace his family's heritage in front of his family, family-to-be, and friends. Mendoza says he has asked his parents to help him pick out a barong, an embroidered white traditional Filipino dress shirt. "I suppose I have decided to wear a barong on my wedding day as a way of expressing that I have come to accept who I am...not only accept who I am, but be proud of it," Mendoza says. "I'm finally comfortable with who I am. It pleasantly surprised my parents that I would wear one because they assumed since I am marrying a Caucasian that I would not want my Filipino heritage to be involved. Funny thing is, I haven't really decided to wear it for them. I want to wear it for me."

&

ZINA VISHNEVSKY

Zina Vishnevsky's earliest recollections of growing up in the United States are enmeshed with the Cold War, when, after World War II the United States and the Soviet Union had threatened war against each other.

On the school playground in Columbus, Ohio, it didn't matter that Vishnevsky's parents had fled Communism or that her Russian father had been a doctor for the British Red Cross. The children didn't care that her mother had been a law student, an assistant clerk of courts, and the daughter of a Lithuanian lawyer. Instead, Vishnevsky's grammar school classmates linked her directly to the Soviet Union. She had been called a "Commie," a "Pinko," and a "Russkie," and she tells me there wasn't anything she could do to end the taunts or make the name-callers go away.

Vishnevky's given name, Zinaida, provided grist for teasing, as well. "I was named directly after my mother, so we shared the same name," she explains. "In second grade, some of my classmates taunted me by turning Zinaida [pronounced *Zina-eeda*] into 'Zina eats a big one.'"

Two people sharing the same name caused problems for Zinaida and Zinaida Vishnevsky. She says the U.S. government and local agencies would not issue documents for her, so she and her mother took a bus to the Social Security office to officially change her name to the shorter version of Zina.

Vishnevsky wishes that just solving the issue of her name would have made her life easier at school, but there were other problems. She says that her home-sewn clothes contributed to her being an outcast. "My mother sewed my clothes and the better ones were made from her dresses, turned inside out so as not to show any wear or tear," she recalls. "My mother added decorative rickrack, and that wasn't what the other kids had. They wore lacy frills for everyday clothes, and slacks and shorts to play in. I wore those darn dresses!"

And then, there was the language challenge. Vishnevsky's father educated her in Russian, so that by the time she started first grade, she knew how to read and write, but in Russian, not English. "Soon, I caught up, but there were moments of shame," she says. "Once, the teacher asked me to go to the blackboard and write the 'sh' sound. I did it in Russian, looking like a cursive W. The laughter! Was

I stupid? Even the teacher didn't understand and I was made to stand at the blackboard with my nose in a chalk circle for not being serious with her command."

Russian language lessons continued through high school. Vishnevsky had to attend Russian language classes twice a week after school, and there was homework. That caused problems when friends wanted to socialize. "I once told friends I couldn't come out to play because of homework and they laughed, 'We don't have homework tonight, you dummy!'"

At night, Vishnevsky remembers her mother tucking her into bed and reminding her to study hard, because an education could never be taken away from her. "Study so you don't have to depend on a man like I do," Vishnevsky recalls hearing before drifting off to sleep. "She encouraged my wish to be a reporter, while my father had always wanted me to be a doctor, like him, a third-generation physician.

Little did Vishnevsky know as a young child that those Russian lessons she dreaded would help her get employment as an adult, and to be proud of the work she was doing. In the 1970s, she says she taught English to Russian immigrants in Columbus. "I went to their homes, some to tutor, some to teach," she says. "I also took people to the grocery store for the first time and I remember how a couple from Moscow was so amazed by the number of toilet paper options we have in America."

Today, Vishnevsky lives in Isla Mujeres, an island in Mexico, where she owns vacation rental property. "Even now in Mexico, I keep my ears opened and start conversations with tourists who are speaking Russian in restaurants, on the beach, or at snorkel sites," she says. "It is great fun!"

∽

RISING ABOVE

TONY XIONG

Adversity seems to have been the fuel that has propelled Tony Xiong* in his life in America. One of ten children born to Laotian immigrants, Xiong's story is filled with childhood challenges that include hunger, the lure of gangs and drugs, violence, assimilation, and learning how to rise above it all.

Xiong grew up in a poor Sacramento neighborhood, where he lived in a two-bedroom duplex with his family of 12. He is ninth in birth order and was born in the United States, while four of his siblings and his parents were born in the mountains of Laos.

Xiong tells me his father, Cher, fought on the side of the United States in the Vietnam War. To escape persecution by the victorious Communists, Xiong says his father moved the family to the United States with the help of an American church.

He says his family's life in the United States could not have been more different than the one they had left behind in Laos. Xiong's parents had been uneducated farmers in Laos, a country where the Hmong people view the father as the patriarch of the family; where families belong to clans; where villages are self-governing; and where it is acceptable to practice a religion that includes animal sacrifice, ancestral worship, and using opium for medicinal and mental health purposes.

Culture clash is what Xiong remembers in his neighborhood, because his parents brought many of their values and traditions to the United States — values and traditions that he says most Americans do not understand. "My dad was a shaman and he would practice voodoo rituals, conduct animal sacrifices, and smoke opium," he explains. "There was a lot of noise and the neighbors would complain and they would call the police."

Xiong recalls an incident when the Sacramento Police Gang Task Force arrived at the family's home to unexpectedly check on his brothers, who were on probation and parole. "My father had his opium pipe set up where he would lay down and when the task force members saw it, they confiscated all of his opium supplies," Xiong says. "They assumed my father was an addict and instead of sending him to jail, they guided him into rehab. Little did they know, the opium use was not just my father's addiction. He used it for traditional purposes as part of his being a shaman, a role that is very respected in our culture."

Xiong adds that because his parents did not speak English, it was extremely difficult for them to learn how to handle everyday living. He says it was hard for them to gain an understanding of American laws, customs, financial requirements, and transportation options. "My parents relied on their children the most to become interpreters, to provide information about American ways, and to supply some financial support for our everyday needs because we lived on welfare," Xiong explains.

When he was young, Xiong says he became embarrassed when his parents could not speak English. "All they knew was to nod their heads and put on a smile, saying one or two words about a situation," he recalls. "I hated it because people would look at my parents and think they were dumb and we would get looked down upon and receive poor services in places like grocery and clothing stores. These are people who were bright enough to use natural resources to survive in the wilderness in Laos, but in the United States, they were treated like idiots!"

Even though he was born in the United States, Xiong says he feels like people don't see him as an American. Because of his looks and the slang he uses, Xiong says some people assume he doesn't speak or understand English well. "I have been looked down upon as a criminal, gang member, drug dealer, high school dropout, on probation or parole, etc., which really I am not," he shares. "I have been stopped by the police when I've been driving my car just to be asked about possible gang activity."

Xiong knows all too well what gang membership and a life of crime can do to a family. Two of his older brothers have been gang members. "Most of the time, they had day jobs and at night, they would steal cars," he says. "They used the money they made from the stolen cars to help support the family."

He specifically remembers one Christmas when his brothers broke into a car and stole wrapped presents. "They became our presents for Christmas and while it was a bad thing, at the time, it felt like a good thing," he says. "The realities in my poor neighborhood were that stealing gifts, cars, and car parts, etc., was a way of becoming and having something that you would not have had if you did not steal it."

Xiong also remembers his brothers stealing a bicycle for him to ride to school and to patrol the street to be a lookout for approaching police so that he could tell his brothers to get out of the house before they arrived at their doorstep. It was his way of trying to protect them and something his gang-member brothers expected of him.

Once, when there was a drive-by shooting at his home, Xiong recalls chaos. When the police arrived, there was an immediate language barrier, which caused much confusion. He remembers two of his brothers being led away in handcuffs and his mother crying and saying to them in Hmong, "Why are you doing this? We raised you to go to school and become somebody — not to become gangsters!"

He adds that as a child growing up in America, he had a big dream. "I always dreamed of being in a white family, because it was much easier and they had everything they needed and did not have to worry about anything," he says. "I know it was foolish thinking of me, but that is what I dreamed of."

Xiong's father died unexpectedly when Xiong was in eighth grade. It turned his life upside down. He adopted a new resolve — to create a better life for himself and to honor his beloved father. No longer would he get bad grades and skip school. "The main message I got from my parents was to focus on school because education was very important to them for a good life in America," he says. "Although they didn't understand the importance of having an education for themselves, they knew how it could open the doors for their children and it could help put food on the table."

Food wasn't always easy to come by for Xiong and his large family. He tells me there are Hmong markets that allow people to buy food based on a promise that they will pay for it on the first of the month, when the welfare checks arrive. "My family relied much on this program in which my parents had sacrificed losing face in the community for going through this program to support our family," Xiong says.

Today, Xiong lives with his eldest brother, who took over the care of his six younger siblings when his father died and after their mother married into another family. "My father taught us that no matter what, a family should stick together," Xiong explains. "My brother did not let my mother take the children because of that."

Xiong has more than enough to eat and plenty of clothes to wear these days. The owner of two cars, he is employed full time by a bottling company as a merchandiser who conducts store inventory checks and stocks shelves. In addition, he is a senior at California State University, Sacramento, with a major in criminal justice and his eye on becoming a police officer. "When I was growing up, when the police came to our house often, I noticed there never was a Hmong officer among them. It was always white officers or those from other ethnic groups," he says. "I want to go into law enforcement to lend a helping hand to my community and others, and to reach out to young adults like my brothers to help make a positive difference."

Because of his experiences, Xiong tells me, he relates well with children from his old neighborhood. "I understand how they feel," he says.

While Xiong has friends from many different ethnic backgrounds, he says he has had trouble trying to fit in with native-born Americans with English-speaking parents. "It's harder for me to communicate with whites because I feel like my English is not as good as theirs, and because it's hard to connect because our backgrounds and struggles have been so different," he says.

Xiong hasn't given up hope, though, for connecting in the future. He says he's working on improving his communication skills so that people don't jump to the wrong conclusions about his being either "too ghetto" or a gangster.

On the flip side, Xiong is also devoted to learning as much as he can about the Hmong culture. On behalf of his family, he attends Hmong events and he is learning as much as he can about rituals from his community's elders.

Xiong considers himself to be Hmong and he is also proud to be an American. "I am glad that I grew up in the United States because here, you basically have everything you need. All you have to do is find a job, work, save, and build a future."

∽

*Tony asked that a different first and last name be used because of safety concerns.

DOROTHY MITSU TAKEUCHI

As I enter the sliding glass doors of the assisted-living home for seniors, I notice a sea of sofas and wooden tables on the vast carpeted floors, and a large fish tank in the middle of the room. Far in the back left corner I see my friend, Judy Gee, who is waving to get my attention.

When I reach her, I see her smiling, gray-haired mother, Dorothy Mitsu Takeuchi, sitting on a fluffy fabric-covered couch. Takeuchi is dressed in tan pants, a green sweater, and a green-and-white-printed blouse. She is 86 years old, and remembers many things with clarity — especially the time when her family was separated and sent to Japanese internment camps. But I get ahead of her story.

Takeuchi's parents were born in Japan and she was born in Seattle, Washington. During her life, Takeuchi's mother, Teru, spoke Japanese while her father, Motosuke, spoke Japanese and English. He had been a graduate of a Japanese agricultural college. Takeuchi says her parents had lived comfortably in Japan but were in search of better economic opportunities when they decided to come to the United States.

Her father operated a wholesale produce company and had employed eight people.

Takeuchi grew up on Beacon Hill in Seattle, a prestigious, predominately white middle-class neighborhood. Named Mitsu at birth, Dorothy had been added as her first name by a church religious leader during her baptism.

Takeuchi attended public school and says she had three groups of friends — white friends in school, white children in the neighborhood, and Japanese friends at her Methodist church.

Her parents had made it a priority to keep her in touch with the Japanese culture. She says her parents sent her older sister, Rurie, to Japan to learn the traditional Japanese tea ceremony and flower arranging, and Takeuchi had been expected to do the same. In addition, her mother was a Buddhist and prayed every day. Takeuchi says she knew that when her mother was praying and chanting, she was not allowed to interrupt her.

She adds that because of Japanese tradition, her eldest brother, Tatsuro, was "the king of the hill" in her family. Having that position, Takeuchi says, he was afforded many more opportunities than the other children. He was able to go to college, own a car, and fly an airplane. Takeuchi resents the unfairness of it and voices her regrets about not being able to attend college. "My father said that girls don't go to college," she tells me.

In happier memories, she says her family always celebrated the Japanese New Year and other cultural holidays when she grew up in the United States. Takeuchi's eyes light up as she recalls precious and beautiful dolls that her mother owned and stored in a special cabinet. They were in the image of the emperor and empress of Japan and the empress' ladies-in-waiting. She could only touch them on the Japanese celebration of Girls' Day, and then they were placed with much care back into their special storage spot. Those dolls brought Takeuchi joy and wonder when she was little and confusion and heartache when she was older.

Takeuchi's parents, like other minorities who were considered "non-white" by federal law (the Naturalization Act of 1790), were not allowed to become citizens, but their children who were born here automatically were. She remembers her parents' emphasis on assimilating in America so that the children would not appear to be different from their classmates. They also expected their children to respect elders, be polite, and make good choices so that their actions would never shame the family.

After Japan's bombing of Pearl Harbor on December 7, 1941, life changed dramatically for Japanese immigrants and their American-born children. Takeuchi remembers the day her high school principal instructed all students to report to the auditorium for an assembly. "We were told that the United States was at war with Japan," she says. "I was afraid to go to school the next day because I was embarrassed. I knew everyone was going to be looking at me."

Fear and rumors of Japanese sabotage spread like wildfire on the West Coast at that time. Major newspapers and magazines incited the public by using racial slurs likes "Jap" in their headlines, and some storefronts featured signs that read, "No Japs."

Hostility and hatred against the Japanese turned neighbors and friends against them. Rumors spread that FBI agents were hunting for Japanese families that might be guilty of sabotage. Takeuchi remembers her mother's fear and tears as she quickly gathered the precious Japanese dolls and threw them into the basement furnace, burning them to remove possible suspicion. "What she told us was that they could be perceived as our being more loyal to Japan," Takeuchi tells me in a softer voice. "When I was 16, the FBI came to our house and found a magazine in the fire and asked about an item that had been circled. It was just a recipe."

On February 19, 1942, President Franklin D. Roosevelt issued an order that required the removal of all residents of Japanese ancestry from their homes and confined them in relocation camps. About 120,000 people were imprisoned, two-thirds of whom were American citizens.

She remembers three polite FBI agents who showed up at her front door at 6:00 a.m. one day. They wanted to talk to her father. "He was one of the first to be interrogated because he was a prominent Japanese businessman with eight employees in his wholesale produce company, and could speak English, which authorities feared would help him become an interpreter for Japan." She says the federal agents took her father away that day without explanation and Takeuchi says they did not know where he was for three years.

When I ask Takeuchi to recall emotions and conversations of that day, she cannot remember. Her daughter Judy interjects, "The Japanese culture is to be proud and not to show emotion; to be stoic and reserved."

Takeuchi does remember a government-ordered curfew. "At 10:00 p.m., everyone had to be indoors with lights out and our shades pulled down," she recalls.

Takeuchi says her three siblings — Tatsuro, Rurie, and Yoshio — and their mother read on posters fastened to neighborhood telephone poles that people of Japanese ancestry were to report to a certain place at a certain time for relocation. "They told us we could take one suitcase and our mother let us decide what to bring," she says.

She also remembers strangers knocking on the front door with greedy intentions. "They asked if we had anything to sell and they wanted it for nothing," she says. "My mother had an old set of porcelain china and someone offered $5.00 for the set. She was so offended by the outlandish price that she threw the china onto the floor because she didn't want them to have it."

On the day of their departure to an unknown location, Takeuchi remembers, "We got into a car and we ended up in Minidoka, Idaho."

"We lived in barracks; the whole family in one room. In the middle, we had a rope and over it, we threw a green blanket to create some privacy from my brothers," she recalls. "I was not angry back then. I did not consider myself an enemy of the country."

Takeuchi says her life at the interment camp was made easier because she had a job as a switchboard operator.

After about three months at the internment camp, Takeuchi says a letter arrived from her beloved father. There was much excitement as the family gathered together to read the long-awaited and precious words on the paper. Her mother cried as Takeuchi interpreted from English to Japanese. "We knew the letter would be censured by the government and saw cut-out holes on the page where there were references to his location, the number of people there, and the weather," she explains. "He mentioned what he was doing and what he ate. He was fine. He said he had enough to eat and that because he was an interpreter for the U.S. government, he had extra privileges, including getting cigarettes."

It wasn't until Takeuchi's father joined his family in the Minidoka camp in Idaho (about two years after they arrived) that they learned of his previous internment. Like others identified as "enemy aliens" by the U.S. government, they were imprisoned in Missoula, Montana.

The forced internment of the Japanese ended in January 1945, about a month after the U.S. Supreme Court ruled that the detainment of loyal citizens was unconstitutional.

Takeuchi was the first of her family to leave the camp after accepting a clerical job offer in Philadelphia. She later sent for her parents and younger brother to live in an apartment near her. (Her brother, Tatsuro, had a job in Philadelphia, too, while her sister Rurie got married and moved to Detroit.) In the so-called City of Brotherly Love, Takeuchi met her future husband, Takeo, who had been in the Poston Internment Camp in Arizona for approximately two and a half years.

"He had the same experience and we talked about it and exchanged information about what we did each day," she says. "We never cried about it. I am not bitter. It was just life. There was nothing you could do about it."

Takeuchi followed her husband to Sacramento, California, where he joined his family in the farming business. Together, they raised four children. Did they speak about their years and experiences in the camps? "Never," she tells me. "It was too painful and too shameful. We were not considered Americans even though we were born here."

Several times during the interview, Takeuchi lets out a slight laugh when she recalls the painful memories. "Why do you laugh?" I ask.

"What do you do when you are too sad to cry?" she responds. "My life has been fine except for one period during the war."

"Do you think something like this would ever happen again in America?" I ask her.

"Yes," she immediately responds. "I am thinking about the Muslims because they are being maligned. We didn't have anyone to stand up for us at that time and if something did happen now, I think most Americans would not stand for it."

"Do you consider yourself an American, a Japanese American, or what?" I inquire.

"I think of myself as an American first, of Japanese ancestry," she says.

∽

FREEDOM RINGS

HENRY PEREZ

Like some of the people I have interviewed for this book, Henry Perez is someone I have not met face-to-face but would be honored to do so in the future. He lives in Miami, Florida and our interview is conducted over the telephone. Perez's story is more complicated than most of the others that have been done so far, largely because of his being an immigrant, a child of immigrants, and someone who entered the country illegally.

Perez, who is 55 and now an American citizen, was born in Cuba. He is a customer service manager, and his appreciation for life in America is strongly linked to his family's experiences in Cuba under Fidel Castro's Communist rule, and to the perilous journey he took to get into this country. "We never agreed with the Castro government and how it treated people in unequal ways," Perez tells me. "Because of that, we were outcasts in our society and we were not allowed to speak our minds."

When he was 5, Perez says his father, Enrique, left Cuba for New York City. "He figured he'd venture into a new life and he promised to try to get us out of there," Perez explains. "I only remember him being there and then gone, but he would write to me and tell us that he was working two or three jobs to get money to bring me and my mom to be with him."

In addition to the letters, Perez's father sent packages from New York. "When we got them, I felt so privileged because he sent us food," Perez recalls. "I got chewing gum, too, but had to secretly share it because if the government found out, we would have been ridiculed and our lives would have been made even more miserable."

When Perez attended school in Cuba, he says the government brainwashed students. "If a child decides his family does not support the government, he could turn them in and become a ward of the state," he says. "So in school, I lied and said we all love Cuba's Communist ideals."

Perez, who lived with his mother, America, Aunt Rosa, Uncle Pablo, and maternal grandmother, Consuelo, remembers seeing them cry often as they worried over the political unrest in Cuba. Other members of his family, he says, supported the Castro regime, and that added to the tension and the caution that was taken when speaking against the new government, even behind closed doors.

When Perez was 11 and his mother informed the government of her future plans to visit her husband in the United States, Perez tells me the government forced her and his uncle to work in internment camps, leaving him behind with his aunt and grandmother. "My mother was put there for two years and my uncle was there for five, and they had to pick tomatoes and other vegetables," he says with anger and sadness in his voice. "She had been a city girl, and had worked in a factory making brand-name bathing suits and undergarments before the government forced her into the countryside."

By the time he was 13, Perez and his mother followed plans his father made for them to travel to Mexico so they could enter the United States as soon as possible. "It was not a happy thing when we left, especially for my mother because of her family and the support group we had there," he says. "We also left behind all of our possessions and when we got to the airport, the guard made my mother give him her wedding ring and another ring my father had given to her as a gift."

By the time they arrived at a Mexican hotel, Perez says they entered a room filled with other refugees. "Some stayed at the hotel for several months, but we ended up staying there for a whole year," he says. "During that time, my mom couldn't work and I couldn't go to school because of the Mexican government's rules pertaining to refugees."

After his mother couldn't get visas for both of them, Perez decided to cross the border illegally and thought he could send for his mother after he settled down. "I was 14 and grew up fast!" he recalls.

Leaving his mother behind, Perez was smuggled out of Mexico in a car and ended up in Houston, Texas, and lived with a minister and his family. "I was in a house of strangers but they treated me very well," Perez says.

After a month in Houston, Perez traveled to Miami where some of his fraternal relatives lived and agreed to take him in. He tells me that in his culture, it is normal for families to live together and to take care of each other.

When Perez started middle school, there were many other Cuban students there, but unlike them, he knew little English. "It was difficult — a different language, new kids, new teachers and everything," he says. "Unlike the restrictive regime of indoctrination in Cuba, I got to look at a normal book and use my mind and my words."

He also points out that in the United States, people can grow up to be whatever they want to be. "In Cuba," he says, "the government tells people what the country needs them to be."

While school was important to Perez, he says his main concern was his mother and making arrangements for her to join him. "I missed her and worried about her being alone in Mexico," he says. "She was my focus and I was relieved when she arrived in Miami about four months after I did."

Because of all Perez and his family sacrificed to come to the United States, he says he feels privileged to live in the United States and appreciates life here much more than others who didn't go through what he did.

Perez says some of his Cuban friends now show resentment toward him because he sees himself as an American first. "I am an American. This is my country," Perez says. "I love Cuban food and Cuban coffee, but I don't follow the Latin culture as much as American culture. My friends accuse me of betraying and pushing away my Cuban heritage."

But those friendly disagreements are okay with him, Perez says. "I am a Republican and most of my friends are Democrats, so we don't agree on a lot of stuff," he says. "That's one of the beauties of this country; we have the freedom to agree to disagree."

∽

ANGELO SPATARO

"Look for an old, balding guy with gray hair. I'll be wearing jeans and a 'MID-TOWN' hooded sweatshirt," Angelo Spataro tells me via email, so that I can recognize him when we meet for an interview at a local restaurant in midtown Sacramento.

That sweatshirt made it easy to find him, but as far as the "old, balding guy" goes, the description is not entirely accurate. He's trim and fit and looks 20 years younger than his 82 years.

We sit at a corner table for two by a sunny, big window in the bustling restaurant. Soft-spoken, Spataro patiently answers the many questions I have for him.

The son of Italian immigrants who came to the United States as a child, Spataro remembers growing up in a family that lived just above the poverty level in an Italian neighborhood in South Rockford, Illinois, outside of Chicago. "I liked where we lived," he tells me. "All of my friends were Italian except for one kid in school, and I'm still in communication with Clinton Verstynen today. Clinton is Dutch and we've been friends since the fourth grade."

When the young Spataro would visit Verstynens' house, he said his friend's family was very welcoming and he noticed that they were better off financially than his own family was. "They had a house, while we lived in an apartment," Spataro explains. "Clinton had his own bedroom. In our apartment, my brother and I shared a bedroom and it was located between my parents' bedroom and the kitchen."

Spataro recalls his family using the roof outside a second-story bedroom window to keep food cold during the winter months. "We had easy access to our milk, meats, and other perishable foods, and during the summer, our perishables were stored in the refrigerator case in the grocery store next door."

The Spataro apartment included a bathroom, but unlike the modern conveniences of today, their galvanized iron tub was in the kitchen. "We had to boil water for the tub, and I usually took a bath first and my younger brother, Sam, would take one after me and use the same water I did," he recalls.

While Sam took seconds in the bathtub, his four-year-older brother Angelo was first in line for family obligations. "In our culture, the oldest has responsibility for the rest of the family," he explains. "I was a baby sitter for my brother and as I grew older, I was expected to provide income for the whole family. That's the way it was."

Spataro explains that when he was about 10 years old, he swept the floor and polished shoes in a shoe-maker's shop on Saturdays for 15 cents a day. "That amount sounds so ridiculous!" Spataro says. "Back then, though, movies cost ten cents and I bought popcorn for a nickel."

While he doesn't remember ever being hungry, Spataro recalls Spartan breakfasts consisting of a bowl of coffee and milk with some bread mixed in. The fam-ily ate a lot of pasta when he was growing up, Spa-taro says. He also remembers the times when his father would bring home live chickens, slaughter them, and turn over the job of pulling off the feathers to his wife, who did so while boiling them in a big pan of water. Spataro tells me his mother was a good cook and did wonders with food — even with dried cod, which they often ate on Fridays, when Catholic families like theirs were forbidden to eat meat. "My mother learned to cook Italian ethnic foods from her mother, who was a very good cook," he adds.

He also remembers a mother who was quick to defend him and also to punish him if he got into trou-ble. Case in point - Without asking, an 11-year-old Spa-taro and a young friend climbed a pear tree to take some of the ripe fruit that was owned by a widow who lived next door. "The next day, the widow knocked on our door and accused me of taking pears, whereupon my mother adamantly denied the accusations, saying her son would never do such a thing," he recalls. "I denied this heinous act, and when the widow produced a hat she found in the tree with my name inked in it, my mother responded to me with a high-pitched lecture about the evils of lying and stealing and how that could make me grow up to be a criminal."

While Spataro's mother stayed home to care for the children, his father worked various jobs, including as a barber and digging ditches for public works projects that were constructed under the Works Progress Administration (WPA)'s jobs program that put millions of Americans back to work during the Depression. "My father only had a third-grade education," Spataro explains. "He was industrious and did what he could to feed us, but it was hard for him to find good-paying jobs."

Spataro was so conscious of his family's uncertain finances that even today, he remembers income and expense numbers such as his father's earnings of $52 per month at his WPA job, and the rent costing more than a quarter of his take-home pay. "I was made aware of that by both of my parents," he says.

By the time Spataro was 16 in 1943, he was earning money for his family by working in a nuts and bolts manufacturing business, thanks to the machinery operation job skills he had learned in high school. "I was hired to work two hours every day after school," he recalls. "I was told I'd make 60 cents an hour and was instructed not to tell the other workers because I'd be making more than some of them were."

Spataro says that kids and women were encouraged to work while so many American men were fighting in Europe during World War II. "In the summer of my senior year of high school, I worked the overnight shift at a machine shop and made $750 for ten weeks of work," he recalls with pride. Spataro remembers turning his paycheck over to his mother. "Whenever I needed something, my parents would get it for me," he says.

Upon graduating from high school at the age of 17, Spataro joined the Navy. For two of his three years in the Navy, Spataro went to school full time to build upon his electrical engineering skills. "I learned how to service and repair electrical equipment like radar and radios," he says. "I spent a year on the Philippine Islands working at a Navy radio station, which communicated weather conditions to ships at sea."

Following his Navy service, Spataro lived again with his family, this time in Sacramento, where they had moved to be with some of his mother's extended family and where his father had the possibility of landing a railroad job. His mother worked in the Libby cannery in Sacramento to help ends meet. "I lived with them until I was 24," Spataro says. "I left because I got married and I had a family of my own to support."

Looking back at his youth, Spataro says his parents didn't speak much about their lives before arriving in the United States from Sicily. He knows they changed their given names of Raimondo and Isabella to Raymond and Elizabeth, but not why or when. As far as his being named Angelo, Spataro tells me it's Italian tradition to name children after beloved family members, so he was named after his paternal grandfather, while his brother Sam was named after their maternal grandfather. "I didn't like being named Angelo," Spataro recalls. "It means 'angel' and I thought it was a sissy name. I wanted to be named Joe or Peter. As I matured, I decided that's the name that was given to me and what could I do?"

The Spataros' cooking ability and last name are well-known in Sacramento, thanks to Angelo's son, Kurt, who is an accomplished executive chef and owner of several of the city's popular restaurants. On June 4, 2005, Spataro Restaurant and Bar was opened, and its menu has been based on recipes that Kurt learned during his travels to Italy when he worked in a restaurant in a small town near Venice. Some of that recipe-learning was during trips Kurt had taken with his father. "It's every parent's wish that their children do as well as or exceed their own successes," Angelo Spataro says. "I appreciate what good people my children have become and am glad they are connected to their Italian heritage. I am especially proud of the

success Kurt has achieved in the food service industry, and of my daughter Kim's success in her job as a
supervisor for the California Public Employees' Retire-
ment System."

In addition to traveling to Italy with Kurt, Spataro
has also made several visits with Kim, and his daughter-
in-law, Kitty O'Neal. "I just love it there!" he tells me.

Angelo informs me that he and his wife, Mary
Anna, are planning a trip to the Northern part of Italy
soon and as part of their preparations, they're learning Italian. A regret Spataro has to this day is that he
didn't learn Italian while growing up. "My parents
were proud of their Italian heritage and participated
in Italian social clubs, but they only spoke English in
our home," he shares. "It was a problem when we visited my mother's parents on weekends and holidays
because they only spoke Italian, and while I understood what they said, I couldn't talk with them."

Spataro is determined to pick up as much Italian
as he can from the CDs he and his wife are listening to.
They're also planning to tour the area and learn from
the locals.

He has fond memories of a previous trip to Arag-
ona, Sicily, where he spent much time looking for and
finally found the church where his grandparents had
wed. His grandmother had told him about the church
and its many steps to the doorway. Spataro found it,
but couldn't go in because it was closed. When he

spoke with villagers there about his grandparents being married in the church, Spataro says they were very friendly and welcoming.

When people ask about his heritage, Spataro says he considers himself to be Italian and also adds that he's thankful that his family emigrated to the United States. "I believe this is the greatest country in the world politically, economically, and regarding our living conditions, as well as its beauty 'from sea to shining sea'," he explains. "I have traveled to Italy several times and enjoyed each visit, but it is always great to come home because I am also an American."

∽

CULTURE CLASH

MAGGIE KAFATI

"We understand Arabic, but we don't speak it," Maggie Kafati, the daughter of Palestinian parents, tells me. "My father tried to get us to write and read Arabic, but he gave up on us. My parents didn't raise us with much tradition since they came to the United States."

The owner of a vintage clothing shop in downtown Sacramento, 28-year-old Kafati stands behind the long glass counter where her mother, Madlen Saba, sits at the far end.

Our talk turns to politics and violence in the Middle East. Her mother shares, "It's not the people who are the problem. It's the government."

A smile grows on Kafati's attractive, brown-haired-framed face as her mother openly speaks her mind.

Kafati tells me her parents met in the Palestinian town of Beit Jala and moved to Honduras in the late 1960s, when fighting intensified between the Arabs and the Israelis.

When they had trouble conceiving, the couple moved to New Orleans, Kafati says, where her maternal uncle, Jacob, lived and health care for infertility was available. "They ended up having six kids in seven years," Kafati, who is third in the birth order, says.

Kafati remembers a Jewish friend taking care of her and her siblings when her mother would go into the hospital to have another child. She also adds that her family observed Greek Orthodox Catholicism.

While Kafati says her parents didn't raise the children with much tradition, she does remember that some of their attitudes about how boys and girls should behave or conduct themselves became a sore spot between them. "They wanted us to grow up as they did in the 1940s and '50s," Kafati explains. "We weren't allowed to go to the movies or the malls with friends or by ourselves, play sports, or be on the cheerleading squad, and it was hard for us. They stopped us from having experiences we should have had when we were young."

Kafati remembers her mother telling her that because of her own upbringing, she believed her children would bring shame to the family if she and her siblings behaved like the other American children. "But we're Americans!" Maggie says was her constant battle cry for independence from what she believed were her parents' outdated and unrealistic expectations. (She confides that the three eldest children were the least successful in getting their way, while the three younger ones were victorious.) "The older ones were the guinea pigs," she remarks.

Kafati adds that the public school she attended had a very diversified student body. "Where I grew up, there were lots of Mexicans, Asians, and different cultures, so being a child of immigrants was kind of normal," she explains.

She says she took in stride some teasing about her bushy eyebrows, including remarks she recalls like, "'Your eyebrows are so big, it looks like you have an eagle on your face' or 'They connect like a caterpillar.'"

Kafati also remembers some kids making fun of her last name, wondering if she was related to Moammar Qadhafi, the late ruller of Libya. "You look like a terrorist," some would say.

Today, Kafati is married and the mother of three children, two boys and a girl. They live in Rocklin, a Sacramento suburb where there is little diversity.

Her children don't have the same kind of rules she grew up with regarding extra curricular activities. "I let my kids play sports and go to all the dances," she says.

Arabic is rarely understood by her children, Kafati says. "It gets diluted with every generation," she observes.

She does try to instill some connection to her heritage through food. "We all get together regularly to cook an Arabic meal and the kids learn from watching. It's the only tradition we really have," she says.

Kafati says one thing that hasn't change since her youth is the angry reaction her father has to television news. She says he curses at it because the war-torn country he and his wife left continues to be such a hot-bed of violence.

∽

MUFADDAL EZZY

It's probably safe to say that when Mufaddal Ezzy was being kicked out of a San Francisco Bay Area middle school for a run-in with a fellow student, no one was thinking, "I bet this kid is going to grow up to become a peacemaker."

But, that's exactly what's happened.

Ezzy, who was raised in Fremont, California to devoutly religious parents from Mumbai, India, says one example of peacemaking is when his Muslim community travels for religious pilgrimages via the San Francisco International Airport. He says he has served as an intermediary between his community and the airport's top brass. Ezzy explains that security checks and tempers are on high alert as travelers are searched for possible terrorist connections. "What do you expect?" Ezzy asks his fellow travelers. "Answer their questions and don't argue with them. We want to travel on safe planes, too."

He says he's humbled and honored to arrange a meeting with San Francisco International Airport executives to help them know when travel by the community will be made to hopefully make things run more

smoothly. He offers explanations, educational litera-
ture, and pictures that show what happens at the religious events abroad. Peacemaking. Understanding.
Conquering the Great Divide. Whatever you want to
call it, Ezzy has succeeded by offering an olive branch.

He does the same kind of thing in his job at the
State Capitol in Sacramento. Take the time he advo-
cated on behalf of Jewish students who were having
trouble convincing University of California administra-
tors that requiring dormitory check-in during the Jewish
High Holidays was a very bad idea. Ezzy, 31 years old,
is a policy consultant for Senate President Pro Tempore
Darrell Steinberg. His duties include helping advocate
for the Senator's constituents.

Ezzy is passionate about his work, his faith, and his
family. He is bursting with childhood memories like the
ones involving his struggles to find his own identity in
America.

He speaks English, Hindi, and a version of Gujarati,
and can read and write Arabic. "I consider myself eth-
nically 'Indian' but am Muslim by religion," he says. "I
am the youngest and most spoiled of three, the most
extroverted, and willing to push the envelope on fundamental attitudes."

Ezzy grew up in a predominantly white neighborhood, attended diverse public schools, and gravitated
to the white students for his friends during his younger
years. "There was something different about them, a

difference that was incredibly intriguing and interesting," he recalls. "Their parents seemed so 'cool' and open. It seemed like they had so much more freedom."

Except for some occasional teasing about his name (and constant mispronunciation), Ezzy found elementary school to be a pleasant experience. He says being a child of immigrants, however, put him at a disadvantage at times, like when his parents didn't know what could cause him problems at school. "When my parents bought me generic crayons, I'd become the butt of jokes by kids whose parents bought Crayolas," he remembers. "My parents spoke English well, but I often served (and still serve) as a translator or interpreter of American popular culture concerning things like jokes or references in American TV shows."

Middle school proved to be a much tougher challenge for him. Ezzy tells me he "freaked out" his parents and contributed to their gray hair when he decided to start more proactively asserting what he believed to be his "American" self. "Priorities were different. I was home at a certain time every night to pray," Ezzy says. "Other kids spent their free time changing the oil in their dads' cars while I was with my dad and community changing light bulbs at the Mosque. That difference was often difficult because nobody outside the community really knew, cared about, or understood what I was in my community."

Even though he grew up with messages from his parents to take advantage of the opportunities that America afforded and not to make waves, Ezzy says he became a "rabble-rouser" in middle school. "It was the early 1990s and dominating the mainstream was gangsta rap and culture, Snoop Doggy Dogg, Dr. Dre, and Coolio," he says. "*In Living Color* and *Beavis and Butt-Head* were the shows everyone talked about at school."

Ezzy shares that he and his best friend started wearing gangsta-type flannel shirts and buttoned them up to the top, even on the hottest days of the year. "I started to think I was real tough," he says. "Even though I had solid grades and pulled my weight academically, being a cool, wannabe gangsta and acting out at school was a convenient way to assert what I perceived to be my 'American' identity."

He says he was able to use his sense of humor to get out of uncomfortable situations, like when a fellow student would tease him about not shaving the "peach fuzz" beard that was growing in. (Ezzy explains that in his Islamic community, men do not shave their beards.) "One kid said, 'So, are you not able to afford a razor?' and as much as it hurt, I would say, 'No. I can't afford one. But, my birthday's coming up. Why don't you buy me one?'" he relates.

One day, Ezzy says, he'd had it with a fellow student who had continuously been teasing and kicking him under the desk, and his teacher wouldn't do anything about it. "The student and I got into a tussle in front of the principal's office and I beat him up," he recalls. "He ended up in the hospital for a few days. It was terrible and stupid." Ezzy admits. "I had to go to Saturday detention at school. They took into account that I didn't have any past problems at school."

Ezzy says his parents also added punishment at home, including forbidding him from hanging out with friends, using the telephone, or riding his much-loved mountain bike. Then, there were the reminders of lessons he was supposed to have learned by now. "They shouted at me for how stupid and dangerous my action was," he says. "They also said that I should know that hurting another person was against the fundamental values we believe in."

About a month later, Ezzy says he and his best friend decided to start a pocket knife business by buying a few at the flea market and selling them at a mark-up at school. He had a knife in his pocket the day he got into an altercation with another student on the walk home from school, and he decided to open and close the knife as an intimidation tactic. "Before I knew it, there were about 30 kids around us, watching. The next morning the school's Vice Principal pulled me out of first period and took me to her office," he recalls. "She calls the cops, pulls in some students and my parents are called," he says as the tone of his voice gets higher and the words are coming faster. "My mom comes, crying, saying things like, 'What happened to my son?' and 'Where did we go wrong?'"

Ezzy says his father was working at the time but when he got home, "I got royally yelled at. My father said things like, 'Do you have any idea what you've done?' and 'Have you lost your mind?'"

Ezzy says that at the time, he thought it was "kind of cool" to get all of that attention and that all of the trouble he got into improved his perceived tough-guy reputation at school. However, when the school moved to have him permanently expelled, he had to appear before the school board with his exasperated and embarrassed mom. (He says his father couldn't' get the day off of work to attend but that he anxiously awaited word on the events and outcome.) "The board members asked me questions, nodded their heads, and told me I really screwed up," he says. "I remember my parents not knowing how to advocate on my behalf, not understanding what their (or my) rights were. I ended up being enrolled in independent study at home for the rest of eighth grade and the first part of ninth grade."

When he was allowed to attend high school, Ezzy says he had seeming "automatic coolness" among peers because of his expulsion. "Getting kicked out of school had a weird way of being good for my reputation," he says as he recalls one student saying, "Whoa, dude, what happened to you, man?"

After tenth grade, Ezzy says his life changed for the better after his parents sent him to Mumbai to work on a business project with one of his father's old friends. He was 16 and stayed with relatives for a year. "It opened my eyes to a whole new world, and I came back to the United States with a new outlook and perspective on things," he tells me. "I had more confidence than ever, was more socially and politically aware, and I was cooler than ever to my peers!"

College was also a turning point for Ezzy. He majored in American Studies at the University of California, Santa Cruz. "For me, it was a place to open up and assert my 'true' American identity, unlike elementary, middle, and high school, where, for example, staff wasn't sensitive to my religion or culture and often lectured me about how taking days off for holidays, that didn't fit neatly within the Christmas break, would adversely impact my work," he explains. "In college, there were these crazy, open-minded students and faculty who would say things like, 'Oh my gosh, you're Indian and you know about incense, and wow!' I told them, I had super incense that wasn't from the head shops they went to but I had the actual stuff from India. It was uncool in college to be seen as fitting within the mainstream definitions of "American" that I had tried so hard to project when I was younger. It was an environment outside my Islamic community that valued, accepted, and embraced 'who I was' and it helped me develop confidence in myself as an American who is distinctly Indian and Muslim."

Sometimes, though, Ezzy says he has had trouble "getting" some American humor, puns, and norms, — something that he attributes to learning about American culture at school rather than at home. He shares an instance concerning how people dress. "I was working in Congressman Sam Farr's office while in college, and no one in my community or at home wore suits," he tells me. "My mentor at the office said, 'Dude, what's up with the white socks? Your socks are supposed to be the same color as your pants. I'm taking you shopping.'"

"I didn't know," Ezzy explains. "Though, all the while, I was among the best- dressed within my community — the whitest, crispest cultural attire, the best-starched Islamic hat," he recalls.

Ezzy also knew that politics was not a career path that he was expected to take. "Politics was something to be watched on the news by us," he explains. "It was for 'other' people to be involved in and to figure out, not us."

Instead, Ezzy says, his parents' generation expected their children to become engineers or doctors, like they were. "They fundamentally came here to make money and have a higher standard of living. They expected their kids to follow in their footsteps and not deviate into unchartered territory." he explains.

Because he chose his own career path, Ezzy says he is honored to often serve as the "go- to guy" in his Indian/Muslim community, because he can get connections made and problems solved.

That doesn't mean he's turned his back on what he's learned growing up. He says for him, America is many facets coming together. "Instead of seeing it as a melting pot, I think of it as a salad bowl," he explains. "There's some Indian spice, a little Middle Eastern culture, some of this, some of that — all of it in there together, part of the universe of distinct things that come together to form a person's own identity while maintaining the individual characteristics of each ingredient."

Ezzy has learned that not everyone is so accepting of that fusion of flavors. "I worry about being hurt in these post-9/11 crazy times," he says and shares a story to illustrate the fear. Ezzy says a few months before I interviewed him, he was crossing a street near the Capitol in downtown Sacramento, dressed in a charcoal, pinstriped suit with his black laptop bag hung from his shoulder. A pick-up truck with two men in it approached. "I thought they were slowing down to let me cross at the crosswalk," he recalls. " Instead, one of them sticks their head out of the window and screams, 'We know what you have in that black bag, you terrorist,'" as I was thinking, 'Man, what just happened?' they drove away and I felt my sense of power and confidence leave. I wondered, 'What would've happened if they had pulled out a gun and shot me? Would someone have stopped and picked me up?'"

Until this story was relayed to me, I had received my information from Ezzy via email or the telephone, but I decided to meet him to see why anyone would mistake him for a terrorist. I was even more dumbfounded when I met him, a trim, light- olive-skinned man, with short, black hair and a beard that appeared to be cut short, even though he showed me that its length is invisibly tucked under what the eye can see. He could be mistaken for having many different cultural heritages in his background.

Ezzy is proud of the person he has become and continues to honor his culture. He is married to a daughter of Pakistani immigrants and they have two children — a three- and- a- half- year- old boy and a daughter who is almost two. "Many of the customs and traditions we had instilled in us growing up, I see myself instilling in my kids," he says. " We strictly observe religious holidays, customs, and traditions. My wife wears a *rida* — a colorful, more expressive version of a burqa. We gather with families from our community often for prayer and meals, and we frequent the Mosque I grew up in, even if it means an almost two hour drive to Fremont."

He remembers his father saying, "Western culture to potlu ghar naa bahar muki ne, ghar ma mumin tarike daakhil thavanu." Translation: "Leave the Western culture in a bag outside the house and enter the house as a 'mumin' [reference to his Islamic sect]." "I didn't understand it as a kid, but it was my mom and dad's way of using the home as a place for the family to maintain our strong values and to embrace our American identity as Muslims and Indians," he says.

Ezzy tells me his parents would be happier if he lived in the same home they did, but he has decided that for the moment, living in Sacramento is a better fit for him and his career. Ezzy speaks proudly about his parents and shares that they were among the first in his community to emigrate from India to the San Francisco Bay Area more than 45 years ago. They continue to have an open door for others who travel from their native country to America. To this day, his mother visits babies and their mothers in the hospital to be an advocate and a guide. Also, his father continues his work helping with the burial rights for every individual who passes in the community.

Like his parents, Ezzy has made a life for himself in America, mixing all of the flavors that his heritage and his birthplace have had to offer. "I had my fair share of ups and downs growing up, but reflecting back, those experiences have equipped me to help my kids and new immigrants better navigate the complex and challenging road to achieving the American dream," he says.

JUDIE FERTIG PANNETON

I have saved my story for last, realizing that it is easier to be an observer than a participant. Sometimes, looking into the past takes an act of courage to dig up memories that mix the good with the bad in order to find some hard-earned wisdom.

While I am a child of immigrants, with my mother, Esther, from Poland and my father, William, from Holland, I have most often viewed myself as a child of Holocaust survivors. It has played such an immense role in my parents' lives, and like second-hand smoke, it has swirled into my life, as well.

I grew up in Kingston, Pennsylvania, in a community where my father worked as a laborer in a furniture factory and later as the owner of a store that made draperies, slipcovers, pillows, and the like. By the time I was in high school, the store went belly up and my father used our basement to produce the custom-made home goods that people had ordered. My mother was a stay-at-home mom, who showed her love through her cooking, cleaning, and prodding so that my older brother, Jim, and I would behave ourselves, do well in school and accomplish goals.

As an adult, I am able to see that picture with gratitude, but as a child, I would have preferred to have been a member of another family. It's easy to feel guilt for saying that now, but it is the truth.

So, truth be told, when I was young, I never wanted to be a child of Holocaust survivors and immigrants. It would have been easier, I had thought, to be like our neighbors, who appeared to live more carefree lives.

I deeply loved my parents, but for me, it was painful to see my father with a permanently inked number on his arm because it spoke of cruelty, hatred, and punishment and it represented the deaths of my grandparents, aunts and uncles, and countless relatives. I had wished that somehow, I could have erased what had happened to my parents, to take away their pain, and to bring back the relatives I never had the opportunity to know.

When I was about 8 years old, I remember sitting with my father on the front, gray-painted wooden steps of our family home. My neighborhood friend, David, came over and sat on the step below mine. He looked at my dad, who was wearing a short- sleeved shirt on that hot, summer day and asked, "What is that number on your arm?"

I silently gasped and felt my heart pound as our eyes settled on my father's pained face. "It's my phone number," he responded, his voice sounding like there was a boulder in his throat, as he quickly changed the subject and it was never mentioned again.

Meal times could also prove difficult in my house, where emotions could flare at the placement of a dinner dish. My mother would serve us each evening at our Formica, kitchen table. I remember one time when my father started eating his meal quickly, his face so close to the mashed potatoes that the steam spread everywhere, as my mother shouted, "Willy, you're not in a concentration camp anymore! You don't have to eat so fast!"

Instantaneously, I bolted from that table in tears, and quickly ran upstairs to my bedroom, and crouched behind an upholstered chair, waiting for the pain and my watery eyes to stop flowing.

Some times, when our supper was done, I'd go next door to join the Mitchell family when they had their dinner. it wasn't for the food, but rather, the nourishing experience. The family of four children and three adults, including a paternal grandmother, would eat at a leisurely pace at their formal, dark, wooden dining room table. The only raised voices were ones of excitement during discussions about daily activities and politics.

Outside of my home, I lived a "typical" American life, attending public schools, joining clubs, and becoming a high school cheerleader. In addition,

I learned how to read Hebrew at after-school classes and worshipped at our Temple.

In 9th grade, I started dating Hani Ahmad, a Palestinian-American, who lived in Forty Fort, a community a few miles away from mine. It never occurred to me that our relationship would be a big problem. During one heated argument with my parents, I remember yelling at them as I raced out the door, "Why did you come to America if you didn't want me to be able to date whoever I wanted?"

Even though my parents objected to my relationship with Hani, they allowed me to use their car to see him.

It wasn't until after I became a reporter for WKXL radio in Concord, New Hampshire that I had an opportunity to interview my father for a profile series that was broadcast. The program taught the station's listeners and me about my father's bravery, how determined he was to survive the daily hell of concentration camps, how he had gratitude for just a piece of potato in his watery soup, and how he had always dreamed about moving to the United States.

The interview also opened doors to more conversations with my parents about their lives in Europe, their tenacity to survive the Holocaust, how they fell in love, about their arrival in America, and the factory work they had to do to earn a living.

The more I learned, the more my pride grew for my family and for my heritage.

Today, I realize that my roots are not connected to the countries in which my parents were born; rather, they're to the spirit of overcoming struggles, the ability to rebuild shattered lives with hopes and dreams for the future, to rise above the hatred and share love, and to raise children to become moral, hard-working, contributing citizens, who actively promote accepting people for who they are.

Each year, I carry our family's stories with me when I speak to students about my parents and about our American experiences. I look at the students' young faces, many of them reflecting their own immigrant connections. I hope that my lessons are registering — to take pride in living in such a wonderful country, to not take its freedoms for granted, to see each other in one another, and to speak against discrimination because It is every American's responsibility. It's what our country is all about and we are all part of its colorful fabric.

ꝏ

PEOPLE IN THE NEWS

When you read the upcoming pages, you are likely to recognize many of the names on them.

Their stories are based on research and they are listed alphabetically.

ANDRE AGASSI

Former professional tennis player Andre Agassi was born in Las Vegas, Nevada. His father, a former Olympic boxer, is from Iran.

Before retiring from tennis, Agassi won an Olympic gold medal, earned eight grand slam titles, and won 869 matches.

In an interview with Terry Gross on National Public Radio and in his book, *Open*, Agassi said it was his father who pushed him into tennis, a game he had come to hate while excelling at it. Agassi told Gross that his father always felt like the world was against him. He said part of that was due to his being a Christian raised in Muslim-dominated Tehran. According to Agassi, his father spent much of his youth fighting in the streets. In addition to religious differences, Agassi said his father had been bullied when he had to wear hand-me-down girls' clothes to school as a punishment by his mother.

Agassi has related that his father believed that tennis would lead him to the American dream and to the ability to have many choices in his life.

In addition to his success in the tennis world, Agassi married another tennis star, Steffi Graf, who, like Agassi, has retired from the professional tennis circuit. In addition to playing tennis for exercise and charity events, Agassi has built a K-through-12 public charter school to benefit children in an economically-challenged part of Las Vegas, Nevada.

∽

CHRISTINA AGUILERA

Christina Aguilera is an award-winning singer and the daughter of immigrant parents. Her father, Fausto, was born in Ecuador while her mother, Shelley, is a native of Canada.

Aguilera was born in Staten Island, New York, but also grew up in New Jersey, Texas, Pennsylvania, and Japan. Aguilera is estranged from her father, an Army sergeant, whom she claims abused her when she was a child. According to an interview with the TV entertainment show *E!*, Aguilera said, "Growing up, I did not feel safe. Feeling powerless is the worst feeling in the world."

She says she turned to music as an outlet for her pain. According to musicianguide.com, her favorite childhood songs were from *The Sound of Music*. Aguilera gained singing notoriety as a teenager after being a member of *The All-New Mickey Mouse Club* and after singing the national anthem at major league sporting events. Her big hit "Genie in a Bottle" sent her to the top of the music charts and has won many honors, including Grammies, and VH1, radio, and Teen Choice awards. She has also been named the World

Music Awards' best-selling Latin female artist, was the host of the Latin Grammy Awards, is a movie actress, and appears as a judge on the television hit *The Voice*.

Aguilera is the mother of a son, Max.

&

TANI CANTIL-SAKAUYE

"She is the living embodiment of the American dream," said California Governor Arnold Schwarzenegger in July of 2010, when he nominated Tani Cantil-Sakauye to be the new chief justice of the California Supreme Court. Cantil-Sakauye is the daughter of two farmworker immigrants and is the first Filipina American judge to be confirmed for the high-court job. (The chief justice of the California Supreme Court is responsible for one of the world's largest state court systems that has more than 1,700 judges and a $4 billion budget.)

Cantil-Sakauye grew up in Sacramento and during her legal career served as a trial judge for 14 years on the California Court of Appeals.

Cantil-Sakauye credits her mother for encouraging her to excel in school and for helping her believe that she has been capable of doing anything in her life.

She is married to a Sacramento police lieutenant, whose Japanese American parents were interned during World War II. They have two children.

Speaking of her nomination to the chief justice spot on the California Supreme Court, Cantil-Sakauye said of her children, "They have a set of grandparents who worked in the fields. They have a set of grandparents who were interned for four years...and their mother? Isn't history remarkable?"

∽

CONGRESSWOMAN SHIRLEY CHISHOLM

"I stand before you today as a candidate for the Democratic nomination for the presidency of the United States," said Shirley Chisholm on January 25, 1972. The first African American and the first woman to launch a presidential campaign in America, Chisholm was born in Brooklyn, New York to father Charles of British Guiana and to mother Ruby of Barbados.

Chisholm, who served as a New York congresswoman from 1969-1982, unsuccessfully tried to win the Democratic presidential nomination, but she opened the door for others with her attempt. She says she ran because someone had to be the first. She thought that most people did not believe that America was ready for a minority candidate to run the country. Chisholm's childhood was not an easy one when she was being raised during the Great Depression. Because of financial difficulties, her parents sent her and her two sisters to Barbados for their early education and where their grandmother could take care of them. At the age of 10, she returned to the United States to rejoin her parents, and graduated from Brooklyn College and

earned a master's degree in early childhood education from Columbia University.

Throughout her life, Chisholm earned many honor-
ary degrees and awards for her political and community work.

In the documentary *Chisholm '72*, she said, "When
I die, I want to be remembered as a woman who lived
in the 20th century and who dared to be a catalyst of
change."

She passed away on January 1, 2005.

∽

MARGARET CHO

Award-winning comedian Margaret Cho, a child of Korean immigrants, describes herself as "the quiet kid who never fit in to any cliques" in high school. Born in San Francisco in 1968, Cho grew up in a racially diverse neighborhood in a city where her parents ran a bookstore, and where she attended a performing arts high school. She started performing standup comedy when she was 16 in a club above her parents' bookstore.

As a standup comic, Cho has made jokes about her Korean upbringing as well as her struggles with her identity and with drugs and alcohol. In 1994, she starred in an ABC sitcom, *All-American Girl*, which focused on the main character's life with her Korean family.

In addition to being a comedian Cho has many other job titles, including actress, writer, gay rights advocate, and political commentator, and she has appeared as a contender in the TV show *Dancing with the Stars* (2010).

In her life and work, Cho advocates for people to feel beautiful just because of who they are.

STEVEN CHU

Steven Chu, the son of Chinese immigrants, is the first Chinese American to be in charge of the U.S. Department of Energy.

Born in St. Louis, Missouri and raised in Garden City on New York's Long Island, Chu is a Nobel Prize winner in physics. He and colleagues at Bell Laboratories earned the prize for their research that developed methods to cool and trap atoms using a laser, which resulted in advances that helped the field of medicine.

According to www.about.com, Chu's parents came to the United States from China in the 1940s to study at the Massachusetts Institute of Technology. They stayed in the United States after their studies because of political unrest in China during World War II. When they moved to Garden City shortly after Chu's birth, they were among the few people of Chinese descent who lived there.

Chu, who comes from a long line of scholars, has held several prestigious positions In addition to being Secretary of the U.S. Energy Department. He has been a physics professor at Stanford University, a researcher with Bell Laboratories, and director of the Lawrence Berkeley National Laboratory in California.

ANN CURRY

Ann Curry is an NBC correspondent and is the former co-host of NBC's *Today Show*. She is the eldest of five children born to Hiroe and Bob Curry. Her mother was born in Japan and her father, in America.

In a *Guideposts* article, Curry explained that her parents met after World War II on a streetcar in Japan, a country where her father was stationed while in the Navy.

Curry credits her parents for being inspirations throughout her life. In the Guideposts interview, she said her mother persevered during adversity including enduring war-time bombing raids, starvation and tuberculosis as well as racism when she arrived in the United States

Curry remembers her mother advising her: "Never give up, even and especially when there's no chance of winning."

She also recalls her father telling her that while life as a mixed-race child in a family of limited income could be difficult, he added that people are made stronger after trials and tribulations.

The advice clearly paid off as Curry grew up and met challenges as a child and as an adult.

With Curry's father serving in the Navy for almost 30 years, the family moved often and they lived in several countries, including Japan and Guam, and in several American states, including California, Hawaii, Virginia, and Oregon.

She and her father were the first in their families to attend college, and they did so at the same time. She worked her way through the University of Oregon by performing such jobs as a hotel maid, a bookstore clerk, and a sandwich maker.

She got her first break in television as an intern at KTVL in Medford, Oregon, where she had once been told that she could never become a reporter because women lacked news judgment. Not to be dissuaded, Curry convinced her boss to give her a chance and she became the station's first female reporter.

Curry joined NBC News in the 1990s and has spent years doing humanitarian reporting around the world. She has said her mission has been to go to countries where there has been unimaginable suffering to report on the hope that rises from the ashes. "I have faith that once you hear about someone's suffering – even someone whose language you can't speak, whose customs you don't share – you will care enough to help," she says.

During a *Today* show segment about searching for her geneological roots, Curry traveled to her mother's birthplace in a rural farming village in northern Japan. It's where she learned from a cousin that her mother had seven siblings and that the family had lived in a one-room farmhouse. Curry said the trip helped her better understand her mother and herself. "Like my mother, out-of-place in America, I struggle to fit in," Curry said in her narration of the videotaped story. "There is much to teach my children."

Curry is married to her college sweetheart, software executive Brian Ross, with whom she has a daughter, McKenzie, and a son, William.

∽

LEONARDO DICAPRIO

Award-winning actor Leonardo DiCaprio is the son of an Italian father and a German mother. According to the website www.imdb.com, DiCaprio's mother, Irmalin, named him after painter Leonardo DaVinci.

DiCaprio, who reportedly visited his grandmother in Germany numerous times during his childhood, was raised by his mother in tough Los Angeles neighborhoods, which he has called "ghettos of Hollywood." DiCaprio credits his mother with getting him into the best schools she could find, and is grateful that both of his parents have supported his career.

At age 5, DiCaprio appeared on the television show *Romper Room,* one of his favorite shows. By the time he was 19, DiCaprio became one of America's youngest actors to be nominated for an Academy Award (for his performance in *What's Eating Gilbert Grape?*).

According to research, he rejected an agent's advice to change his name from Leonardo Wilhelm DiCaprio to Lenny Williams to make it more "American-friendly."

In addition to being an Oscar-winning actor, DiCaprio is an active environmental conservationist and advocate. From a *Parade* magazine interview: "I think I was sort of a little biologist when I was younger. I watched documentaries on rain forest depletion and the loss of species and habitats and it affected me a lot."

DiCaprio drives a hybrid car, has a "green" house with solar panels, and enjoys living a lifestyle that may be an inspiration to others.

෨ჿ

RAHM EMANUEL

Chicago's mayor, Rahm Emanuel, is a child of an Israeli immigrant. The former White House Chief of Staff for President Barack Obama was born in Chicago and his father, Benjamin, is a native of Israel. (Emanuel's mother, Marsha, was born in Chicago.)

He is Chicago's first Jewish mayor and his Israeli and American roots have played a significant part in his life, according to Maureen Dowd's column in the *New York Times*, where the following Emanuel quote comes from: "For me, as Rahm Emanuel, the grandson of Herman Smulivitz, who came to this city in 1917 from the Russian-Romanian border as a 13-year-old to leave the pogroms, and son of Benjamin Emanuel, who came here in 1959 from Israel to start a medical practice, there's a personal sense of accomplishment."

Emanuel is one of three children who grew up in a home where taking advantage of opportunities was stressed along with remembering the sacrifices others have made. According to myfoxchicago.com, "The three sons say their overachieving intensity comes, at least in part, from the photos on the wall of the den in the family's West Wilmette home and to the stories told at that wall by father Ben. He's a veteran of the Irgun, a Jewish paramilitary that helped Israel achieve independence from Great Britain in 1948. Ben Emanuel would use the photos to illustrate Jewish history... and to tell the stories of ancestors who had been killed by anti-Semites."

Following his election, Emanuel told reporters he was humbled and gratified.

His former boss, President Obama, said he couldn't be prouder for his friend and fellow Chicagoan.

∽

DR. SANJAY GUPTA

Dr. Sanjay Gupta, the chief medical correspondent for CNN, is the son of Damyanti and Subhash Gupta, who were born in India and moved to Novi, Michigan in the 1960s to work as engineers for the Ford Motor Company. His mother became the first female engineer to work for Ford.

A practicing neurosurgeon and an assistant professor of neurosurgery (Emory University School of Medicine in Atlanta), Dr. Gupta started working for CNN in 2001, and, according to CNN, his "passion for inspiring Americans to lead healthier, more active lives" has led him to launch programs and initiatives about the American diet and against childhood obesity.

Dr. Gupta served as a special advisor to Senator Hillary Clinton when she was America's First Lady and has been a contributor to *60 Minutes* and the *Evening News* on CBS.

When he married Rebecca Olson in 2004, Dr. Gupta fulfilled one of his parents' dreams by having a traditional Hindu wedding.

෴

NORAH JONES

She's known for her beautiful voice, lyrics, and looks, but many people may not know that singer Norah Jones is the daughter of Indian-born Ravi Shankar, an internationally-known sitar master. She grew up in Grapevine, Texas with her American mother, Sue Jones, and has a deep-rooted identity as a Texan.

According to an interview on *60 Minutes*, Jones says she saw her father several times a year until she was about 9 years old and then not again until she was 18. The media has conflicting reports about the long split, with Shankar saying Jones' mother did not want him to contact Norah. When she was 18, Jones reportedly found her father and met with him and his second wife and their daughter in California.

Katie Couric interviewed Jones in the *60 Minutes* segment, and following is a part of the question-and-answer conversation. Couric: "Do you consider yourself part Indian?"

"I grew up in Texas with a white mother," Jones said. "I feel very Texan, actually, and New York. New Yorker."

Jones has said that she and her father are very close now, even though they live in different parts of the world. In an article in London-based *The Telegraph*, Jones said she had recently visited India for a month, where she saw her 89-year-old father and other relatives. When asked in the interview if she'd like to record a song with him, Jones responded, "'I would love to do it, but I would love to just spend time with him and not put pressure on it for some public reason…'"

Jones started singing in church choirs at a young age and by the time she was 26 years old, she had sold 30 million albums. She has also won five Grammy awards. In an interview with Oprah Winfrey, she said, "… I've had a lot of luck in my life, knock on wood…"

∽

JAY LENO

Standup comedian and former television show host Jay Leno, who was born in New Rochelle, New York and grew up in Andover, Massachusetts, is a child of a Scottish-born mother and an Italian American father. His father, Angelo, was born in New York, the son of Italian immigrants, while his mother, Catherine, was born in Scotland and came to America when she was 11.

According to a book about Leno entitled *Life and Humor*, Leno's father, Angelo, was an insurance salesman who frequently told jokes at sales meetings and often served as a master of ceremonies at company banquets.

Leno has always looked up to his parents and, as a child, had hoped to follow in his father's footsteps as a gregarious salesman and a capable joke teller. When he refers to his parents in jokes or funny stories, it's always in a lighthearted and loving way.

In *Life and Humor*, Leno is quoted as saying, "I come from the kind of family where my mom ironed my socks. In case my shoe ever fell off, people would know I came from a good family."

৩

MARIA MENOUNOS

NBC correspondent and philanthropist Maria Menounos is the daughter of Greek parents and says her family comes first in her busy life. In a *Guideposts* magazine article, she spoke lovingly about her parents and extended family, and recalled holiday gatherings where there was much love and laughter.

She added that she came from a long line of hard workers and recalled how her father had a variety of jobs to support his family, including being a carpet installer and a janitor at a night club, while her mother worked at a school cafeteria.

Menounos said she worked at Dunkin' Donuts to support herself while attending college and later went to work at Channel One News, *Entertainment Tonight*, and NBC.

A former model and Miss Massachusetts Teen USA, Menounos is referred to as a celebrity journalist on some websites. She regularly appears in magazines, on popular television programs in dramatic roles, and has served as a spokesperson for beauty products.

A director and producer of films, Menounos has founded Take Action Hollywood! — a charity whose goal is to use feature films and commercials to educate, empower, and raise social awareness on issues including AIDS and overpopulation.

෮

APOLO OHNO

Olympic speed skating champion Apolo Ohno was born in Seattle, Washington. He was raised by his Japanese-born father, Yuki, who was a hairdresser. Ohno's mother was an American.

According to a *Sports Illustrated* article, "Apolo, a latchkey kid, fell in with a crowd of petty criminals and juvenile delinquents...he dropped out of an honors program in junior high school because his friends thought it was uncool."

By the time he was 14, Ohno had been introduced to the world of speed skating, in which he excelled. His performance at junior national team trials in Sarasota Springs in 1995 was so impressive that a development coach recruited him for the Olympic Training Center in Lake Placid. It was the first time anyone so young had been admitted to the center.

According to the *Sports Illustrated* article, Ohno's father dropped him off at the Seattle airport to take a flight to the training camp but instead of hopping aboard a plane, Ohno picked up the phone and called a friend to pick him up. "'I had it all planned,'" he reportedly related. "'Dad told me, 'I know what's best for you; you need to listen.' He comes from that Asian background; he's strict. But, I'm 14. I don't want to do anything anybody says.'"

Long story short – Yuki eventually ended up accompanying his son on a flight to the training center and the rest is history. Just two years later, in 1997, Ohno won the U.S. championship, becoming the youngest American to ever win the Olympic medal in speed skating.

In 1998, Ohno's performance at the U.S. Olympic trials was abysmal. He finished last in a field of 16. Instead of going home after the Olympic trials, he ended up at a cabin on the Washington coast by himself, to contemplate his life. Yuki's parting words as he drove away, according to the *Sports Illustrated* interview, were, "'If speed skating is not what you want to do, I want to know.'"

Ohno apparently had an epiphany during his time alone: he wanted to take his life and his skating career more seriously.

Ohno ended up winning five Olympic medals during his career.

He also showed his competitive spirit and athletic ability during the TV show *Dancing with the Stars*, when he won the championship in 2007. His father, Yuki, was once again in the audience cheering him on.

DR. MEHMET OZ

Dr. Mehmet Oz, the Emmy Award-winning host of The *Dr. Oz Show*, is the son of Turkish parents. He was born in Cleveland, Ohio and raised near Philadelphia, Pennsylvania. According to www.pbs.org, Dr. Oz's father, Mustafa came from a poor family, while his mother, Suna's family had a wealthier lineage. (In spite of his limited economic means, Dr. Oz's father reportedly excelled in school, earned scholarships, which allowed him to become a medical doctor after being a resident at a Cleveland, Ohio hospital in 1955.)

Dr. Oz, who performs more than 200 heart operations a year and is an author, inventor, and scientist, is vice chair and professor of surgery at Columbia University, and is the New York Presbyterian Hospital director of the Cardiovascular Institute and Complementary Medicine Program. Again, according to pbs.org, Dr. Oz's medical philosophy, in part, has a connection to his Turkish heritage and combines alternative ideas about healthy lifestyle choices with traditional Western medical techniques for treating diseases.

Proud of his Turkish roots, Dr. Oz credits them with having a positive effect on his personal and professional lives. According to an interview with the *Turkish Times*, Dr. Oz is more tolerant of others and believes that non-traditional methods of healing and traditional medicine don't have to be mutually exclusive.

Dr. Oz and his wife, LIsa, have four children: Daphne, Arabella, Zoe, and Oliver.

∽

GENERAL COLIN POWELL

Army General Colin Powell was born in Harlem in New York City to Luther and Maud Powell, who were Jamaican immigrants. He attended public schools and earned a bachelor's degree in geology from the City College of New York, and a master's in business administration from George Washington University.

In an interview with Dr. Maya Angelou on oprah.com, General Powell said his parents urged him to work hard and do well in school. In General Powell's words, "They said, 'You can be a bus driver or you can be a doctor, but in this family, you're going to be something and you're going to make something of yourself.'"

General Powell says his parents' high expectations helped propel him to the type of success that is now legendary. According to an interview on scholastic.com, General Powell was a professional soldier for 35 years. During that time he held many different command and staff positions. His last assignment, from October 1, 1989, to September 30, 1993, was as the 12th Chairman of the Joint Chiefs of Staff, the highest military position in the Department of Defense.

During this time he oversaw 28 military and political crises, including Operation Desert Storm in the victorious 1991 Persian Gulf War. In 2001, Powell became the first African-American Secretary of State, under President George W. Bush.

In the interview, General Powell said it was an honor to be the first African American U.S. Secretary of State: "I also felt a great deal of gratitude towards the black soldiers who had served before me in the past, but because of segregation and racism, never had the chance for themselves to become the Chairman of the Joint Chiefs of Staff. They were the trailblazers for me. It's because of their sacrifices that I was able to get to where I got. And now I want to try to make things better for the young people who come after me.

General Powell has received several military awards, is the author of a memoir (*My American Journey*), and advised four presidents during his long career, including Presidents Ronald Reagan, George W. Bush, George H.W. Bush, and Bill Clinton.

The general has been active in America's Promise Alliance, an organization that provides funding and community support to help give children a "happy, pleasant, secure childhood." In an interview on NBC with the late Tim Russert, General Powell urged national healthcare for children, dedication to helping more students graduate from high school, as well as teaching children the importance of community service.

General Powell and his wife, Alma, have a son and two grandsons.

 managed

MICHELLE RHEE

Education reformer Michelle Rhee is the child of Korean parents and was born in Ann Arbor, Michigan and raised in Toledo, Ohio. The founder of a political advocacy organization, StudentsFirst, she is the second of three children born to Shang Rhee, a physician, and Inza Rhee, a clothing store owner. In addition to attending public and private schools in Toledo, Rhee also attended classes for one year in South Korea. Encouraged to do community service by her father, Rhee worked on a Native American reservation as a teenager.

She earned a master's degree in public policy from Harvard University, taught for three years in Baltimore's inner-city schools, and founded a teacher recruiting and training program called the New Teacher Project. Rhee also served as chancellor for Washington, D.C. public schools, where she earned a reputation for firing alleged incompetent teachers and doggedly pushing for reform.

Rhee has two children and is married to Sacramento Mayor Kevin Johnson.

DR. JONAS SALK

Dr. Jonas Salk, the son of Russian immigrants, was born in New York City in 1914 and will be remembered as the developer of a vaccine against polio, a crippling disease that was prevalent in the 1950s in America.

Dr. Salk's parents had encouraged their three children to study hard and he was the first member of his family to go to college. He had planned to become a lawyer and dreamed of being elected to Congress but chose a career in medicine after his mother convinced him he wasn't good at winning arguments. Dr. Salk attended medical school at New York University.

While working at the University of Pittsburgh School of Medicine, Dr. Salk spent eight years trying to find a vaccine to cure polio. The discovery was made public in 1955 and has been used in countries around the world. Dr. Salk did not patent the vaccine for profit. According to an interview with the Academy of Achievement in Washington, D.C., Dr. Salk answered a question about having a sense of duty to help the world in this way:

"I have the impression that people like that are born as well as made…I think that is something inherited…. Our nature is revealed in the course of life experience, and the nurturing comes from the opportunities that are available. If I were born in some other country, for example, my life would have been quite different."

In addition to being a successful writer and researcher, Dr. Salk had also tried to find a vaccine to cure the AIDS virus.

Dr. Salk died at the age of 80 in 1995.

ᘒ

IVANKA TRUMP

Ivanka Trump was born in 1981 to American real estate mogul Donald Trump, and to Ivana Trump, a businesswoman, former fashion model, and athlete, who was born in Gottwaldov, Czechoslovakia. Ivanka Trump is the middle child in the family. She has a younger brother, Eric, and an older brother, Don.

Trump works for the Trump Organization's real estate interests in the areas of domestic and global expansion as its executive vice president of development and acquisitions. She has appeared with her brother Don on their father's television show, *The Apprentice*.

According to an interview in *New York Magazine*, Ivanka and her brothers were raised with help from two Irish nannies. According to the story's writer, Jonathan Van Meter, "... the most important early influence came from Ivana's Czech parents, Milos and Maria Zelnicek, who lived with the family in Trump Tower for six months out of the year."

Prior to joining the family's real estate business, Ivanka Trump had a prestigious career as a fashion model and earned a degree in economics from the

Wharton School of Finance at the University of Pennsylvania. She continues to be a frequent guest on a variety of television programs and appears in other media.

Trump is married to Jared Kushner, the owner of the *New York Observer*, and they have a daughter. Arabella Rose.

෨

MICHAEL SAVAGE

Talk show host Michael Savage was born Michael Weiner in New York City and his parents, Ben and Rae, were Russian immigrants. According to an article in *San Francisco Weekly*, Savage's father had been a street vendor and eventually owned a small antique store on Manhattan's Lower East Side. The article adds, "Benny had a chip on his shoulder and was always mad at the world, and he was tough on Michael. There was nothing Michael could ever do to please him," recalls Alan Zaitz, who has known the radio talker since the two of them were in Hebrew school together as second-graders.

Savage often weaves stories about lessons he's learned from his parents on his nationally syndicated radio talk show, *The Savage Nation*.

He is the author of 18 books and has master's degrees in medical botany and medical anthropology, and a PhD in nutritional ethnomedicine.

A controversial talk show host, Savage carries a gun and sometimes hires a bodyguard for protection.

MAURICE SENDAK

Author Maurice Sendak (*Where the Wild Things Are*) was born in Brooklyn, New York to poor Polish immigrant parents. According to http://www.kidsreads.com/authors/au-sendak-maurice.asp, Sendak's parents came to the United States before World War II, but had many family members who were killed during the Holocaust in Nazi Germany. Sendak's mother constantly worried about her relatives in Europe while he was growing up, and she worried about him because he was a sickly child.

In addition to being a world-famous author, Sendak has had other talents. He has written lyrics for both an animated television film and an opera based on his classic children's book (and movie) *Where the Wild Things Are*. He has also helped design sets and costumes for operas and has designed wooden toys.

༙

HILDA LUCIA SOLIS

Hilda Lucia Solis is the Secretary of the U.S. Department of Labor. She was born in La Puenta, California. Her parents emigrated from Mexico and Nicaragua. She was the first in her family to graduate from college and is the first Latina woman to serve in the U.S. Cabinet.

In an interview with CNN reporter Brianna Keilar, Solis said that it was a dream come true to serve in the Cabinet and in such a diverse one at that.

Solis was the first Latina woman to serve in the California State Senate when she was elected in 1994. She also was the first woman to receive the John F. Kennedy Profile in Courage Award in 2000. Prior to her appointment as U.S. lLabor Secretary, Solis served in the United States House of Representatives.

In her CNN interview, she related that a high school counselor told her she was not college material and should pursue a career as a clerical staff person. After graduating from college, Solis said she went back to her high school and urged Latina students to put college in their future plans.

ᕯᕯ

GEORGE STEPHANOPOULOS

George Stephanopoulos, the son of Greek immigrants, is the anchor of ABC's *Good Morning America* and the network's chief political correspondent.

Before joining ABC News, he was a senior adviser in the Clinton administration, worked on the Michael Dukakis presidential campaign, served as an aide and Chief of Staff to Cleveland Congressman Ed Feighan, was a professor of government at Columbia University, and wrote a book, *All Too Human: A Political Education*.

Born in Fall River Massachusetts, Stephanopoulos grew up in Purchase, New York and Cleveland, Ohio. His father, Robert, is a Greek Orthodox priest and Dean Emeritus of New York City's Cathedral of the Holy Trinity. His mother, Nickolitsa, worked as director of the national news service of the Greek Orthodox Archdiocese of America. Like his father, Stephanopoulos had considered going into the priesthood and attended the University of Oxford in Oxford, England, where he earned a master of studies in theology.

According to an article in *Time* magazine, "Stephanopoulos developed his selflessness as the grandson and son of Greek Orthodox priests, expected to be above reproach — a child impersonating a grown-up."

Stephanopoulos and his wife, actor Alexandra Wentworth, have two daughters. Elliott and Harper.

∽

AMBASSADOR ELENI
TSAKOPOULOS-KOUNALAKIS

"Although I was born and raised in California, my father, Angelo Tsakopoulos ensured that the history of southeast Europe, and its neighbors, was very much a part of my upbringing," Eleni Tsakopoulos-Kounalakis told the Senate Foreign Affairs Committee during her confirmation hearing on her nomination to become ambassador to Hungary. She is the daughter of Greek immigrants, Sofia and Angelo. Angelo has made a fortune in real estate development in Sacramento and in California.

Tsakopoulous-Kounalakis has been the ambassador to Hungary since 2009. She was nominated for the post by President Barack Obama. Prior to becoming ambassador, Tsakopoulos-Kounalakis served as the head of Greek Americans for Hillary Clinton's presidential campaign, and as president of AKT Development Corporation, one of California's largest land development firms. She attended undergraduate school at Dartmouth College and earned a masters in business administration from the University of California, Berkeley. She is a philanthropist and has served on several government panels, including the World Conference of Religions for Peace.

She is the mother of two sons and is married to Markos Kounalakis, the publisher of the *Washington Monthly*, who is also a child of Greek parents. Kounalakis' father, Antonios, fought against the Nazis during World War II.

∾

HINES WARD

It was hard for Steelers receiver Hines Ward to find his identity and to make friends when he was growing up in Georgia as the child of a Korean-born mother and an African American father. "The black kids didn't want to hang out with me because I had a Korean. The white kids didn't want to hang out with me because I was black. The Korean kids didn't want to hang out with me because I was black."

Ward, named the most valuable player in Super Bowl XL, has turned that childhood pain into a drive to succeed on the football field and as an advocate for those who have been discriminated against because of their bi-racial heritage.

He carries a central message with him and shares that he understands all too well what it feels like to be on the outside looking in. His message: never be ashamed of who you are and embrace the opportunity to be part of several cultures.

Each year, Ward helps sponsor several children from Korea to come to the United States so that they can feel accepted and celebrated for who they are instead of chastised, like they have been back home.

It's a great culture," Ward has said. "I love everything about it. But there's a dark side to that culture. And me, I'm trying to shed light on that dark side and make Korea a better place than it already is."

When Ward was named the most valuable Super Bowl player in 2006, some of the anti-biracial attitude dramatically changed in South Korea. Ward and his mother, Young He Ward, went to South Korean so that he could be honored by the country's president. Being famous opened doors for him but he knew many doors would continue to be closed to other biracial South Koreans and he has been committed to working on their behalf.

In the fall of 2010, Ward became the only athlete to be appointed to President Barack Obama's Advisory Commission on Asian Americans and Pacific Islanders. His main focus has been on eliminating the bullying that bi-racial children have endured.

Ward, who was born in Korea, but came to America when he was one, has not forgotten his roots or the sacrifices his mother has made while learning English, working in the school cafeteria, and raising a son to be someone who continues to make a difference around the world.

ᔕᑐ

POSTSCRIPT: PEOPLE POWER

I hope this book has helped you better understand your fellow citizens, who are among a growing group in America's ever-changing demographic.

Because of immigration, the U.S. Census Bureau has predicted that by 2023, it's possible that more than half of the children who live in the United States will be members of minority groups. Come 2050, that number is expected to jump to 60 percent.

According to the study, "Inheriting the City," by researchers at Harvard University and City University of New York, children of immigrants "will not only reshape American racial and ethnic relations but will define the character of American social, cultural, and political life."

I am thankful to live in America and to be surrounded by people with diverse backgrounds.

Judie Fertig Panneton

∾

Author Judie Fertig Panneton is a child of immigrants, who are Holocaust survivors. This is her second book based on a collection of stories. Her first was *The Breast Cancer Book of Strength & Courage*. She is an award-winning journalist with experience as a print, TV, and radio reporter.

For more information, go to :
www.proudamericansspeak.com

Made in the USA
Middletown, DE
14 May 2021